PRAISE FOR LIVE YOUR WHOLE CAPACITY

"A beautifully written and very personal account on how to live a more conscious life.

This book is as encouraging as it is insightful. Written with the warmth, vulnerability, humility and generosity that mirror who Adele is, she offers us what she learnt in her authentic search of 'self' and outlines how to build the capacity for beauty and love in a disconnected and confusing world."

— *Ralf Schneider, founder and Managing Director of Better Business.*

"This is a book of charm and adventure - into a sense of personal wholeness. Adele shares her knowledge and experience of the many avenues to explore, wisdom practices to draw on and the impact it has had on her life. It would be a cheering companion for others on a similar` path."

— *Judith Hemming, founder of MovingConstellations, founding member and faculty at the Centre for Systemic Constellations, and former director of the nowherefoundation.*

"If I presume that I can be helpful to others, I have to do my own work, simultaneously and continuously. Adele's very open story of her journey of learning and growth is a wonderful example of a practitioner's commitment to use of self to support others."

— *Philip Mix, OD consultant, co-founder, faculty and dean, NTL Organisation Development Certificate Programme (UK).*

"Adele has a way of offering multidimensional approaches that generate effective changes for her clients. Adele's presence has a wonderfully calming influence and herbook provides practical inspirations for engaging with one's own inner guide.

What I love about working with Adele is her amazing ability to bridge the organisational, personal and spiritual realms. Drawing from her personal success, this book gives expert advice as well as a treasure trove of professional tools anyone can use to successfully engage with heart in corporate settings.

There is something remarkably kind and warm about Adele's ability to help others enhance their own capacity for change. If you are ready to gently open to new and empowering approaches to personal success in business and in life, then you will enjoy the journey with Adele as you learn how to harness your own unique capacities for optimal living."

— *Amara Charles, author of The Sexual Practices of Quodoushka and founder of Nourishing Arts.*

"Using her skills to effectively work with multi-stakeholders and across institutional boundaries, Adele sparks change that is truly transformational. This book sheds light on how she does this. Adele takes readers on a journey to discover their greatest teacher within. Empowering and inspiring."

— *Martin Kalungu-Banda, leadership consultant, faculty of Presencing Institute, author of Driftology: How to Access Life's Greatest Opportunities by flying on the wings of others.*

"My encounters with Adele were always somewhat magical. To me, she is inspiring as a peaceful warrior for good, a subtle spiritual teacher, a loving mother. Her quest for finding wisdom and sharing of knowledge with others is like a warm light glowing around when you learn with Adele."

— *Miroslava Rusnokova, Head of HR, Exponea, Slovakia.*

"Adele has an amazing ability to awaken you to seeing your life as a intricate and beautiful journey. She is able to connect with people through their life stories and resonate truth. My many discussions, collaborations and incubations with her remind me of two researchers working on a thesis, not using books and articles for data, but delving into one's own life experiences and exploring the capacity for happiness and wholeness. I love the playful exploration of ideas and how she uses her physical and spiritual senses to tap into the power and potential of the natural and emotional world."
— *Monita Sen, Regional Manager -School Services, at the International Baccalaureate.*

"At times delicately but never skipping the need for honesty, Adele invites you into an exploration of her heart and mind. It is this journey that compels the reader to ask questions that will sniff out the very birthplace of behaviour. Her words coax a sense of intrigue as to the source of all the emergences and disappearances of our various character traits. If you have ever wondered if you had a soul, this is a wonderful place to start looking."
— *Paul Laurenson, behavioural expert and author of The Element of Surprise.*

"Adele has an open, honest, and accessible approach toward living our lives with confidence and integrity. She gently reminds us to dive back into, rather than outside of, ourselves, to access our own wisdom and guidance. This is the resuscitation many of us need. She is also a courageous example who will undoubtedly be a catalyst for many to rediscover their own light illuminating the path they choose to travel."
— *Dr. Nancy Sutton Pierce, clinical sexologist, RN-health educator, international speaker, author, intimacy and health expert, and yoga therapist.*

"This book is such a body of work. If you find yourself reading this now, you are likely a potential contributor in the foundational uncovering of Whole Systems models that bring Whole Capacity about."
— *Pi Villaraza, founder of Inner Dance and co-founder of Bahay Kalipay Detox and Retreat Center, Palawan, Philippines.*

"Adele follows a humanist approach in her work. She cares deeply for people and their development. She respects the individual's path and provides gentle guidance to their own truth along the way."
— *Ksenia Anikina, successful international career woman, wife and mother.*

"Adele Lim has always been thoughtful and delightful. She writes from her heart and her message is enlightening and fresh. Having personally seen Adele grow from a muddled little girl into an amazing women, her sharing of her experiences and journey is a joy to read."
— *Roshan Thiran, CEO of Leaderonomics and Editor of leaderonomics.com*

"Adele is a woman of strength and dignity. She is bright, ambitious and a natural leader. She always follows through on commitments, no matter how small it may seem. And always seeks for ways to help someone and she does it."
— *Pamela Akasha Kaur, co-founder of Almonds and Raisins, certified Kundalini Yoga teacher and Conscious Pregnancy facilitator.*

"Adele is a compassionate kind spirit, giving love and care with all she comes in contact with, always ready to engage with others, and to look at herself. She has a passion to help others to find themselves. I would recommend Adele and her work to anyone who needs some advice or inspiration."
— *Shyena Venice, International Entrepreneur.*

ABOUT THE AUTHOR

Adele M Lim is the Founder of and Lead Catalyst at Whole Capacity, a global web of catalysts working with individuals and organisations to facilitate movement and innovation in change and growth.

With an emphasis on systemic approaches and leading from the core, her work inspires and sustains change on multiple levels. She brings extensive training and experience in leadership coaching, talent management and organisation development, and has served as an internal and external consultant to blue chip multinationals, spanning a broad range of sectors across global environments.

Her application of individual and organisation development practices are grounded in a practical understanding of how things are on the ground.

Adele holds an MSc in Information Management and Finance from University of Westminster, and a Certificate in Organisation Development from NTL Institute (formerly National Training Laboratories of Bethel, Maine).

Her professional training includes Systemic Constellations, Theory U, and the Inner Dance Energy School. She is also a Chartered Member of the CIPD, UK.

LIVE YOUR
WHOLE
CAPACITY

How to tap into and grow
unknown potential
in your life

ADELE M LIM

Copyright © Adele M Lim, 2016
Published by I_AM Self-Publishing, 2016.

Adele M Lim asserts the moral right to be identified as
the author of this work.

All rights reserved.

ISBN 978-1-911079-91-0

This book is sold subject to the condition it shall not, by way of
trade or otherwise, be circulated in any form or by any means,
electronic or otherwise without the publisher's prior consent.

Some names and identifying details have been changed to protect
the privacy of individuals.

@iamselfpub
www.iamselfpublishing.com

While every effort has been made to verify the information here, neither the author nor the publisher assumes any responsibility for errors in, omissions from or different interpretation of the subject matter. This information may be subject to varying laws and practices in different areas, states and countries. The reader assumes all responsibility for use of the information.

The author and publisher shall in no event be held liable to any party for any damages arising directly or indirectly from any use of this material. Every effort has been made to accurately represent this product and its potential and there is no guarantee that you will earn any money or cure from any diseases using these techniques.

For my expansive family... past, present and future.

CONTENTS

ACKNOWLEDGEMENTS 15

FOREWORD 17
    Why I Wrote This Book 21

INTRODUCING WHOLE CAPACITY
    The Key Elements of Living Your Whole Capacity 37

WAYS TO BRING THE ELEMENTS TO LIFE
    Way #1: Getting Unstuck 51
    Way #2: Getting To Know Your Identities 65
    Way #3: Getting In the Flow of Your True Nature 77
    Way #4: Keep Living More Consciously 89
    Way #5: Start Opening Up To Different Choices 99
    Way #6: Opening The Portal Of Sexuality 107

THE PRACTICE OF WHOLE CAPACITY
    Bringing It All Together 123
    Immersive Living: The Practice of Living Your Whole Capacity 129

APPLICATION
    Applications of Whole Capacity 147
    Application #1: Whole Capacity in Business and Organisations 149
    Application #2: Whole Capacity In Intimate Relationships 157
    Application #3: Whole Capacity in Parenthood and Childhood 167

IN CLOSING 175

BIBLIOGRAPHY 177

ACKNOWLEDGEMENTS

In order for this book to come into form, I am deeply grateful to many lives, loves and souls, for the touch, weave and flow, ever converging, diverging or spiralling, in or out of sync.

Specifically between 2007 when this project began, till 2016, I am indebted to these beautiful individuals I shared my life with, for their role and meaningful contributions to my book journey, named here in no special order:

Charles Bentley, Shermaine Low, Ksenia Anikina, Emma Rowlings-Jensen, Helen Read, Francesca Brown, Mee-Yan Cheung Judge, Philip Mix, Martin Kalungu-Banda, Ralf Schneider, Kamlesh Bolla, Oberdan Marianetti, Caroline Horner, Nana Sonaike, Alison Whybrow, Katie Lane, Damian Gardner, Graham Prentice, Judith Hemming, Terry Ingham, Bjorn Thomas Atterstam, Laurence Barrett, Bethan Jones, Miroslava Rusnokova, Danielle Lee, Jeremy Kourdi, Mark Williamson, Laurence Guinness, Yvonne Chan, Hilary Lance, Jack Robertson, Guni Baxa, Monita Sen, Irina Miu, Anutosh Foo, Jean Houston, Ellen Vanhoven, Nigel Wylie, Pi Villaraza, Paul Laurenson, Amara Charles, Shyena Venice, Nancy Sutton Pierce, Lynn Kwek, Pamela Akasha Kaur and Violet Hau.

Last but not least, I am grateful to my second husband for all the gifts that flowed from our relationship, my daughter for channelling unconditional love in mirroring the inner child, and to my parents and brother for standing by me and their unwavering support. Thank You!

FOREWORD

Whole capacity is intrinsically inbuilt in the infant as much as it is in traditional societies, much alike cultures in Asia, where values held in community, family and in all other social dynamics, trust the human being's tacit knowing.

Many Asian cultures traditionally view Wholeness from the lens of the Mandala. A picture that holds that all parts synchronically branch out from a sense of middle; a recognition of the heart of all things as pure and central.

This is the book's central theme. That all parts stem or stream from our heart. And when we find this crux point, order emerges from what often seems chaotic. All of that which invites us to trust that all things originate from one source, as they similarly end in the same irreducible singular place.

What might it mean to achieve Whole Capacity in the age of complexities, of information, of multiple connections? In today's modern era, we do not always have to learn this, as much as we are called to simply remember. And in this, we find that everything we need has always already been within us since birth.

Adele's body of work, in life and in book format, teaches us how the new schooling isn't always creative and constructive. Today, to learn is as much to unlearn what we think we know. We are taught to deconstruct what the Buddhists call Maya, the world of illusion, what the Hindus consider the magical theatre that keeps us all enthralled.

This deconstruction isn't so much a demolition job as much as it is a surgical dissection of our many parts, and how each and every one of these inter-relate with the whole.

Whole Capacity rests in self-sufficiency. To be sufficient, we must self-recognize; the kind of self-recognition that brings about self-love, which then heightens our self-esteem, followed by self-efficacy, and finally, our ability to respect ourselves, as we also believe in our capacity to conduct the passionate visionary work at hand.

We are often tempted to manage the world through resource management. And yet, the integrative spiritual growth path reminds us that in order to be whole, we must tap sources of energy, insight and creativity from within. Resource, in the spirit of deconstruction, is Re-Source. It is a return to Source.

Organizations held by visionary leaders now wonder how Whole Systems will bring about Whole Capacity, not just for a dynamic business entity, but also for each and every member of any self-organizing ecosystem. Nature obviously teaches us how life cycles without effort or force. Spontaneous flow tends to all the members of the system, without the need for meetings, timetables, logistical planning or memorandums of agreement.

The successful organization that thrives in the 21st century mimics nature in all of its essential dimensions. Nature is never driven by need, or motivated by transitory desire. Nature is energetic, it rests in all living and non-living beings. Nature follows natural principles, whatever the situation asks for.

The Principle called Energy Conservation calls forth our expanded at-easeness. In this expanded state, our intrinsic life force needs little instruction. Our bodies heal, our insights arrive and our relationships improve. We see the world as it truly is - sacred and simple.

In this sacred simplicity, Conservation shifts into Conversation. We suddenly hear the deep structures uniquely held in us all, as personality, culture, temperaments begin to move into shared spaces with all the beings we touch and are touched by on a daily dialogic. The Conversations lead to Communion, a long-held dream of inclusive family systems coming true, where every one is our brother, every one is our sister, every one is our father and every one is our mother.

Having witnessed Adele undergo her own personal quest for Wholeness, I was honoured that she asked me to contribute to her work in bringing Whole Capacity to others. Adele has served as one of my intimate teachers of what she teaches through example. When we are lucky enough to encounter such opportunities to learn from these new facilitators of truth, the insights have intuitive dimensions that are abundant and take much time to grasp in linear thought.

It helps us that Adele's life-work marries the east-west paradigms reflected in how different cultures now collide and inter-mix as one emergent world-view. The natural Oriental mindset is group-oriented. Just as the Occidental is inclined towards individuation. At this juncture where Asians learn to develop stronger identity, and Westerners look into the deep value in learning what it means to create stronger community bonds, any single work that elegantly brings both worlds into homeostasis deserves our attention.

Pi Villaraza, Puerto Princesa, 2016

WHY I WROTE THIS BOOK

My journey into writing this book began in 2007 when I left a promising Finance career to move into the totally different field of Human Development.

During this period, I also made the decision to end my first marriage and move to London.

I was turning everything I knew as my life upside down to step into a world that was so alien to me, and where, as the main actor, I was not even sure I knew how to play or be myself anymore.

My search led me to meet some of the most amazing people, including myself.

I felt like I was dying.

Everything I had ever known about me was dissolving, as if being sucked into a black hole. I mourned for the loss of all that I knew about me and what I thought I was pursuing.

In that period, I was like a child learning to stand and walk, and learning the vocabulary and grammar of a strange language, with no reliable past knowledge to draw upon.

On the surface, I looked no different from the many people I commuted to and from work with on every busy working day in the London Underground, and no different from the many people who hung out at cafes, museums and parks at the weekends. Underneath my calm exterior, I was a sea storm. It was the darkest most confusing period of my life.

But something kept me going. I was looking to feel better. Or perhaps I was looking to prove to myself and my family that I did the right thing.

Whatever the case, my search led me to meet some of the most amazing people, including myself; the many aspects of myself, all my co-existing identities.

In seven years, I got married and divorced, left my motherland, changed career, met my second husband, got married, became pregnant, wound up back in Asia, became a mother and transitioned to doing my life's work.

My conscious and unconscious learning from all my life experiences, particularly in those seven years, had begun to form clear patterns and wonderful insights.

I felt excited about what I was discovering and started sharing it with a small circle of friends. Many encouraged me to write about my discoveries but I hesitated.

I hesitated because I was afraid that I was not going to appear technical, intelligent and researched enough. Other reasons were not crystal clear to me as fear is often easily masked by excuses, complexes and doubt:

- "I am too busy and I don't need to share what I learned."
- "No one will listen to me without a PhD."
- "I need to do 'proper' research with big names endorsing it to be worthy of having an audience."
- "Can I really pull this off?"
- "What if I let myself down?"
- "What if I let others down?"

Until one day, I experienced déjà vu.

Dissolving the Old Me

Sharing what I learnt by writing a book was like dissolving me, as I knew me, to step into the unknown. At one point in time, that meant utter darkness, very painful, and very scary.

So I struggled with making progress on the book until I realised that I needed to really connect with WHY I wanted to write the book; the Big Why. What purpose did I want to serve?

As a human and organisation development practitioner in large multinational companies, I was exposed to and had gotten involved with, how things generally operate in large multinationals.

These organisations mostly have a long history behind them, and practices that had kept them going for years. Unhealthy politics and competition were rife.

The big gap between what we know and what we actually practice became an accepted norm. This is one of the common causes of many organisational illnesses and perpetuates an environment of helplessness where innovation is simply stifled.

As a passionate learner with an active-reflective style, I was constantly on-the-go, connecting my various experiences in and out of the office, journaling and meditating.

I felt like I was living multi-parallel lives, spinning many plates, feeling productive and optimistic, but somehow overwhelmed and unfulfilled. I was also worn out from going against the grain and kept thinking that there must be another way; a healthier, happier way, for everyone involved.

Additionally, my constant exposure to both personal development and professional development kept reinforcing my opinion that we cannot split the individual to parts and only deal with the professional one at work.

I was worn out from going against the grain and kept thinking that there must be another way.

When we go to work, whilst we can choose to leave our personal problems at home, for example, systemically they are with us, in our energetic field, and vice versa (we are impacted by the collective energy that exists in the organisation).

And no matter how adept we have become at splitting parts of ourselves and being professional, whatever that means, we cannot ignore the fact that the majority of us will have our experience coloured by both our current state as well as the nature of our whole being.

So who and how we are impacts, and are impacted, by others constantly, whether we like it or not.

I first encountered the idea of the Use of Self as an Instrument for Change when I was on the NTL Organisation Development programme. The theory goes that the only tool anyone truly has to bring about change is themselves, even as a consultant to organisations.

We must choose to use all that we are, past, present and future, to intentionally bring about change.

Live Your Whole Capacity

We must know how to use ourselves as the instrument of change. And to do this, we must own and refine our instrumentality.

To own means to develop self-knowledge and to refine means to engage in regular maintenance work on the self. In other words, if we want anything to change, we need to start with ourselves, in every sense of the word.

- We must know who and what we are, our biases, worldviews, and lens, our motivation, needs and wants, our default tendencies, strengths and weaknesses, and our blind spots.
- We must be willing to continue to grow as a person and be well-resourced for that.

And when we walk into a scheduled or chance encounter, we accept that we are presented with an opportunity to impact another.

With awareness and skilled use of self, we can be more conscious about how to engage and enable a better outcome for all.

Understanding this mapped my work tremendously. Within my contracted capacity, however, I struggled to get traction even if I managed to get people on board with an idea.

I was not placed appropriately in the organisation system to affect a flow of change. I felt like I was forced to play on the surface when I know that to truly effect a change, we all need to work deeper.

I also struggled to shift the mindset of many large Corporates about learning and organisation development; that it is less important to put effort into this, than on departments that worked directly at generating revenue for example.

Yet for companies that did invest significant amounts of money on learning and organisation development, many also fail to support the designed intervention enough and effectively follow through, in order to reap the full benefits of the investment, out of personal and institutional fear.

A Different Person

On December 7, 2011, in London, after watching Tom Shadyac's documentary "I Am," I experienced something unexpected and rather surprising.

As I was walking home from the screening, I broke down. I was shaking. I had to stop walking, bend down to collect myself, and continue walking.

What was supposed to be a 15-minute walk felt like eternity and all I wanted when I got home was to take a warm shower and curl up in bed with sleeping socks and a hot water bottle. I could not find any words to share what was happening with my husband.

> *Despite what I truly and deeply believed, I was feeling victimised and forced to live against my values.*

I woke up the next morning a different person; distant yet connected, alone and somehow in the presence of many, motivated but clueless, sad and calmly joyful, all at the same time. To this day, I cannot forget that experience.

Fortunately, I had a wonderful boss at the time whom I could share such weird stories with, and he said without batting an eyelid, "It sounds like you had a spiritual experience."

Live Your Whole Capacity

It is rare to hear such phrases being uttered in big companies but I was fortunate. I was fortunate because I got the space at work to process what had just taken place, simply because someone who impacts my day-to-day heard me and acknowledged my experience.

With each passing day, it increasingly dawned on me that despite what I truly and deeply believed, I was feeling victimised and forced to live against my values whenever I went to the office.

In fact, I had known that for quite some time but I had either ignored or rationalised the emotions. I had given up my power to live my own life in a fully conscious and immersive way, in partnership with the world.

And I only realised it because that day, I experienced through every inch of my being, what "stop, this is enough" truly meant.

- I could no longer do many of the things I used to do in the same way.
- I could no longer do many things without being concerned about its impact on society.
- I could no longer turn a blind eye on some of 'the way things are'.
- I could no longer ignore the voice inside me that for things to change, I must do different.
- I could no longer collude without feeling responsible and angry about my lack of courage.
- I could no longer pretend that I wasn't colluding by inaction or helplessly following orders.
- I could no longer un-see the ill effects of selfish agendas nor make excuses for them.

- Most of all, I could no longer believe that my judgements make me any better than those I judged... I could no longer separate my parallel lives without compromising my well-being.
- I knew I had to do something.
- And I was willing to make a step change even if that meant massive personal change.
- I just didn't know how... yet.

Seeing Clearly

A couple of years later, a spiritual friend described what happened that night as "Crying for Mother Earth." I began to connect with the world like never before, and to see more clearly than ever that there exists a happier, healthier, alternative way of living life together:

- A life that is lived fully, a courageous and inspired life that is cooperative, collaborative, co-creative and game changing.
- A life that is kinder and more grateful to all participants on a grand scale.
- A life that like-minded individuals who embody such existence can spread like colonies.

I began to see a new reality that is not only an aspiration or possibility, but that it can most likely happen if enough of us choose this to be.

And if human beings are the ones capable of bringing what has yet to be formed into form, then it goes without saying that we are responsible for what is happening in one way or another.

So until we start making different choices, we will continue to create what we have chosen to in the past, consciously or otherwise.

We are part of many interacting systems and we cannot continue to behave as if they do not exist or deny individuals of their right to live their whole being.

I began to see that while frustration can seed a desire for change, it could never be the source power for change.

My sudden allergic reaction to how I had been playing along all my life battled head on with the resentment that I had been carrying and they just did not jive. In the end, the strong energies eventually transmuted and I understood that the source power for change is love... cliché, cheesy, goose-pimply or bone-chilling as it may sound.

This is when I caught up with an old acquaintance who strongly encouraged me to write, and this is why I began writing this book. I realised that the impact of what I share could be profound simply because it came to being out of love.

New Capacity

As if that was not enough, in the midst of consolidating my research and writing up, I became pregnant, became vegetarian and gave birth to my daughter Alis, in my mother region.

Within such a context, her birth and presence added another dimension to how I was experiencing life up to that point. Becoming a mother opened up a whole new capacity in me.

Whether this is described by some as an initiation, a rite of passage, an opening of a portal, or plainly a big change, is immaterial.

Her birth gave me a tremendous opportunity to love, remember and recover, and it gave me fresh "organs" to interact with the world, to elevate and expand both my thinking and ambition.

Nurturing and being with her gave me a chance to understand our inherent ability to be creative and entertain all possibilities. I started to experience synaesthesia; the ability to smell beauty, taste sadness, hear discoveries, touch ideas, feel air and see thoughts.

All the possibilities that she embodied, I experienced. It was exciting and lonely at the same time. I was afraid of talking about it for fear of being judged.

I also began to experience empathy at a totally different level. I would properly tear up with a knot in my heart and stomach, trying to hold back a full-on cry:

- Upon seeing a photo of my friend's daughter at her first prom night.
- On hearing stories of how an orphan's visiting mother ignored her child's request for her to prepare simple instant noodles.
- On touching the scarf my mother knitted for me when I first left home.
- On reading about how insecure fearful crying babies were left to cry it out.
- On hearing about how corporal punishment is still being freely wielded by certain quarters of society who believe it to be the only proven way to raise obedient children.

Personally, this process of growth also entailed experiences of hormonally-charged regressive behaviours. My childhood demons as they say started to show their face in ways it never had before. How I heard my husband, how I perceived his behaviours towards me and my daughter, how I heard my parents and how I perceived their behaviours towards me and my daughter, were constantly shifting dynamically with increasing awareness.

I got to know myself and the hidden beliefs I carried in ways I never knew before.

All of these experiences led me to believe in our tremendous capacity to improve how we live, in every dimension of the word; to live from a healthier, happier place within.

> *I got to know myself and the hidden beliefs I carried in ways I never knew before.*

I have read and heard stories upon stories about the capacity the human race has to overcome adversity, to recover or reclaim our innate ability to live in wellness, but experiencing it for myself through a primal experience of childbirth and parenthood brings a depth of understanding about my discoveries that allows me now to share it in a meaningful human way.

Life Experiences

Like many others on this planet, I too, have numerous sets of powerful life experiences, each bringing its own lessons and enrichment.

I am deeply grateful that for some reason, life brought me to a point where I began to see a pattern emerging from all the seemingly unrelated patches of experiences, as if everything I have ever done has prepared me for today.

I did not get here alone. I never could have made it alone. On some level, I understood that, yet it is the experiences of visiting my past, present and future lives that brought the sense of a moving whole, alongside a web of support.

It was my Whole Capacity that held me through it all; all of me, all of my families and relations, all of my deeply felt connections and bonds. No matter how excellent my families and friends and support network independently are, I needed to corral my Whole Capacity to bring about a change.

I have had to work hard at finding my deeper voice and speaking my truth, and I am deeply grateful to be able to do this today. Yes, I could be more elegant and more perfect but I am and will always be, a work in progress, and I am happy and at peace with that.

My proudest personal work, if you may, is growing into the full adult version of a daughter in the richest sense, growing in my capacity as a wife in its broadest meaning, growing as a mother in her fullest expression, and becoming my own cosmic partner in humble and unyielding co-creation of beauty in evolution.

My intention is to life-dance as consciously and as creatively as I can, moment by moment. I enjoy an expansive life and I love both states of being and creating immensely.

My vision is to live with gratitude every single day, knowing that I am moving while being fully present with life, loving and laughing and infusing my wider web with lightness of spirit, grounding of life-forces and inspirational possibilities from living our Whole Capacity.

In This Book

As we go through this book, I will disclose intimate details of my life as necessary. I will share less client and more personal stories in this book and where client stories are used, they are with full permission to be gifts to all who pick up this book.

I believe that when I am given permission to peek into someone else's life, it is so that I can do my work, and leave.

Feeling honoured and humbled, I trust in my client and the process and often when the work is finished, I forget most of it and only remember what I need to remember, viscerally.

I guess this is what makes it harder for me to write about my clients than it is about my personal experience.

In short, I am here in my Whole Capacity to be of use to you.

I wish for you to experience all positive changes from applying what I share and making yours, what is useful for you, and I hope that these changes have empowering ripple effects into all areas of your life.

Adele M Lim

PART I:

INTRODUCING WHOLE CAPACITY

For more information and special offers, join our community at: **www.WholeCapacity.com**

THE KEY ELEMENTS OF LIVING YOUR WHOLE CAPACITY

It was December 31. I was at my friend Nana's flat to celebrate the countdown.

She was heavily pregnant with twin boys and did not fancy being in the thick of action along the River Thames, so we decided to have our own party, in the comfort of her home, just two couples.

Five minutes before countdown, I had a whim and asked, "If there was one thing you could change in the world, what would it be?"

> *"What a time to ask such a deep question!"*
> *"One thing? That's hard."*
> *"Eradicate illnesses."*
> *"Homes for every orphan."*
> *"Cooperation replaces competition in world economics."*
> *"It's got to be to increase kindness. If everyone was kinder, it will be a different world."*

Then there was a mad rush to get toasting glasses as the countdown began on the television. Soon after the toasting and wishing, we bid our goodbyes and called it a night.

We never got to expand on that particular topic of conversation, as life ran its natural course. But the question stuck in my mind.

Answering the Question

I accept that few of us can change the whole world. But most of us can change aspects of our own world if we choose to.

My experience is that many people do want to change what is going on in their own world.

> *Most of us can change aspects of our own world if we choose to.*

But the truth is, I have seen far too many beautiful, kind and generous people and organisations that live in prisons of their minds and old rehashed stories, afraid of stepping into a new way of being and simply waiting for something to happen or for things to change.

So many of us, with precious unrealised capacities, have at different points in time found ourselves:

- Trapped in relationships or situations where we have a repeating a set of problems or patterns of behaviour.
- Unable to innovate or solve new problems any differently or make progress on certain projects.
- Stuck in a rut or living a life that does not feel wholly theirs, perhaps living an assigned role or somebody else's script.

Live Your Whole Capacity

- Not knowing what we want for ourselves despite knowing what we do not want.
- Creating or perpetuating a stuffy or suffocating environment around us.
- Having little ideas and/or motivation to choose alternative ways.
- Feeling and being helpless yet live in fear of being rendered irrelevant.
- Constantly falling ill or generally lacking in vitality.
- Being addicted to external stimulants for the endorphin and dopamine kick.

Despite that, there are alternatives. And many people know that there are alternatives.

However, this calls for a common understanding that we create our own reality, and many people struggle with that.

I am not saying that we choose all that has happened, is happening and about to happen. What I am saying though is that while we do not choose what has happened, is happening and about to happen, we can choose and create how we experience things.

Since this is both shaped by our lens of the world and how we are with the world in processing our experiences, we can create differently.

In order to step into our powers to do so, we must believe that our reality can be lived through conscious design. This is an important factor in helping us welcome and bring forth alternate realities.

Whether our life is experienced as a prison, or an ever expanding holding space, it is up to us to take that call.

A large part of our experience is driven by how we perceive it internally, and because we are unique, we each experience and respond to our environment differently, even if we live in the same place and complain or concur about the same things.

If you broadly agree with this view, then you will understand that when we change, when we allow ourselves to grow in new ways, our experience of life changes. And because we are unique and live in relationship with others, when we change, the unique way in which we relate inevitably changes too.

In essence, we live in constant interaction with our external environment, and in doing so, we influence and are influenced by our external environment, consciously or otherwise. Therefore, we can architect our internal environment and in so doing, we live from a healthier, happier place, in harmony with all of who we are.

We can become more aware and learn responses that are friendlier to our whole being instead of controlling, wishing, or willing the impulses, feelings or thoughts away.

This is what I mean when I say we are able to live our Whole Capacity.

A New Way of Living

This book aims to open up a new way of being and living. This book is about developing our Whole Capacity as a collection of systems, as an individual, as a partnership, as a community and as humanity.

When asked what surprised him most about humanity, the Dalai Lama answered:

> *"Man. Because he sacrifices his health in order to make money. Then he sacrifices money to recuperate his health.*
> *And then he is so anxious about the future that he does not enjoy the present; the result being that he does not live in the present or the future; he lives as if he is never going to die, and then dies having never really lived."*

Putting the Dalai Lama's message about living and dying into a question:

How can we live happily and healthily, overcome obstacles and relate with ease on a day-to-day basis?

Ultimately, how can we live well, and die well when our time is up?

In this book, I will attempt to present some ways to examine these questions. I will describe the why, how and what of living our Whole Capacity, and through this, communicate why I believe it is our birth right as much as it is a duty of every human being.

What is Whole Capacity?

When I first started talking about Whole Capacity, I often get asked, "Do you mean 'holistic'? Do you mean you include all aspects consisting of the physical, the spiritual and the emotional, in the development of your Whole Capacity?"

The short answer is no. Whole Capacity is not the sum total of our physical, spiritual and emotional bodies.

It includes them all, *and* it also accounts for the unseen and all relationships between them, internally and externally, across space and time, as we relate with ourselves and with others. It is difficult to describe, without sounding woolly.

An old quote once suggested:

"The whole is greater than the sum of its parts".

Conventional wisdom also tells us that there exist relationships and dynamics that dance with everything.

When we include these aspects, we come closer to describing Whole Capacity.

Add to this melting pot, the concepts of embodiment and way of being, concepts that are central to living life more fully, and we begin to speak about the same thing – Whole Capacity.

It is in the embodiment and way of being that is more aware and attuned to the whole environment that is central to living one's Whole Capacity.

When one lives one's Whole Capacity, one is able to take in more data and with clarity, make decisions and take actions that one might not have been able to otherwise.

Live Your Whole Capacity

The Three Elements of Whole Capacity

So, what is Whole Capacity, in a nutshell?

There are essentially three key elements that determine whether we are living our Whole Capacity:

1: Identity

Whole Capacity is about honouring and embracing all our Identities... every single aspect of them, whether those we attach to, those we reject or those that we are ambivalent about.

Through living and working with our Whole Capacity, we go beyond the direct development of the body and mind by opening up a space so that our latent potential and hidden parts of our whole nature is allowed to surface for living.

And unlike making the effort to sharpen our five physical senses, developing our Whole Capacity helps us to 'grow' extra sense organs, extra capacity, to attune to our world and receive fresh data to live, play and work with.

Whole Capacity is about flowing through the dance of our Identities in every context that we encounter.

2: Nature

I call this flow through dance, our Nature, because it has its own rhythm and cycle, and it is the product of this dance that, like the ecology of our existence, brings to life, the essence of life.

Whole Capacity is about allowing ourselves to make new

Choices.

3: Choiceful Creation

Through expanded sensing, we are better able to engage much more with a particular experience, and summon courage to experiment with making new Choices.

I call this Choiceful Creation; the ability to choose deeply and follow through on what one needs to manifest based on fresh data and new choices that are being revealed from living our Whole Capacity.

Understanding and developing ourselves in the context of these three elements is key to living our Whole Capacity and that's what we'll explore as we go through this book.

Singing and Dancing

In 1703, Andrew Fletcher, made an observation which he became famous for:

> *"If a man were permitted to make all ballads, he need not care who should make the laws of a nation. Let who will make the laws of a nation so long as I am permitted to make her songs."*

Loosely translated, music and lyrics can shape a nation much more effectively than any law ever will.

In practice, we accept that songs are the artistes' creative form of expression.

Live Your Whole Capacity

So when the songs resonate and we allow an artistic piece to penetrate through our pores, the artistic piece turns into a form of open-ended therapy and a way of expressing our core.

When they don't resonate, we tune out, and an effort is made by the listening body to shut the song out.

However, everything we take in, consciously or otherwise, choicefully or in protest, shapes us.

Everything we take in, consciously or otherwise, shapes us.
And we in turn shape others and their world.

And as we engage with others in our world, we in turn shape others and their world.

There is research that suggest even our thoughts impact others in the vicinity.

Therefore, is it not our duty to choose well the songs we sing, literally and figuratively?

And so, if living our Whole Capacity means we are living with all of who we are in the best possible way as much and as often as we can, i.e. singing our ideal songs, then wouldn't we be increasing our chances of living happily and healthily whilst performing our duties without even so much as thinking about it?

Experimenting

We can experiment with and expand our Whole Capacity by:
- Getting to know our Identities.
- Exploring our Nature.

- Reflecting on Choices that have been made or surfacing Choices that are about to be made in order to manifest or create in a choice-full manner.

Developing our Whole Capacity can be undertaken as a conscious intervention, or simply experienced through a series of life events taking its course, providing we give it space to integrate.

It is my intention that by the end of your sojourn with me in this book, you will receive what you need to receive, and develop practical ideas for growing your Whole Capacity. And that perhaps you will return to the elements in this book again at a later time, as you evolve your personal growth practice.

I cannot claim credit for much of the work here in this book, save for the personal research and extensive life-work integration that had kept me busy for over a decade.

I am also not suggesting that Whole Capacity is the next wave to get into, for the idea is not entirely new. What I am stating with this book is that a practical way of developing our whole being is absolutely necessary and here is one way to look into this and lovingly make it applicable.

How this growth process is expressed varies from person to person.

Fundamentally, a deeply felt and embodied appreciation for who, what and how we are, where we have come from, how we are now, and where we are going, is the essence of living our Whole Capacity.

I invite you to discover, in your own way, what Whole Capacity means to you.

Live Your Whole Capacity

This capacity to engage ourselves and others without getting sick, self-righteous, paralysed, overwhelmed, or disconnected, is our birth right. By living our Whole Capacity as often and as best we can, we are enabling a healthier world, starting with our own personal world.

We live from a healthier, happier place than when we don't live our Whole Capacity, and the more we can do that, the more we can enable that in our world.

Defining Whole Capacity any further this early on limits the depth of meaning behind that phrase. It needs to be personally experienced to be taken in, digested and expanded.

So I invite you to turn the pages and discover, in your own way, what Whole Capacity means to you, and how this may serve as one of your catalysts for growth.

May you find your voice and sing your song in an even more powerful way than today.

PART 2:

WAYS TO BRING THE ELEMENTS TO LIFE

For more information and special offers, join our community at: **www.WholeCapacity.com**

WAY #1: GETTING UNSTUCK

Have you ever wondered why...
- You do certain things and think that you have no other choice?
- Why something insignificant to someone else could bother you so much that you lose sleep, patience or centeredness?

In these instances, do you wish for something to change, anything but yourself to change?

Or on top of that, you doubt and blame yourself and others too?

Have you ever experienced a knowing that you want things to be different but cannot see why, how or what, to bring about something different?

If you ever feel like this, you are experiencing what I like to call, the Stuck State.

Experiencing the Stuck State

Whenever we experience such a state, it is a sign that, at that point in time, we are not living our Whole Capacity.

Many of us long to get unstuck, even when we know that everything may well settle in its own time.

Sometimes this Stuck State manifests as going in circles, i.e. moving from Stuck State in an attempt to get unstuck but somehow reverting back to being stuck.

We may find ourselves in a constant dilemma, flipping back and forth between different courses of action, never really making a commitment for change, or end up repeating patterns that no longer serve us.

Sometimes it shows up as a big gap between what we say and what we do, compromising our ability to live our lives authentically.

There are times when we do not even know we are in the Stuck State.

Then there are times when we do not even know we are in the Stuck State.

We are either too busy or too tired to notice, or too angry or afraid to realise that we are actually driven by something deeper that is beyond our control.

We may be afraid of discovering new things about ourselves and shy away from activities that involve active self-inquiry, experimentation with the self, participation in individual or group therapy and other human development workshops that can bring out energetic, emotional and psycho-spiritual patterns and imprints, to get to know and integrate.

We say things like:

> *"I don't need it, there is nothing wrong with me."*
> *"It's spooky/touchy-feely/not my thing."*
> *"It doesn't work for me, I'm too logical."*

> *"There is no point opening a can of worms when we cannot solve everything."*
> *"I don't have time for such self-indulgence and navel-gazing."*
> *"It's too expensive."*
> *"My partner is not supportive."*
> *"I have my religion or faith and that is enough."*

And then there are others who become development 'junkies', going on workshops after workshops for a 'fix', forever "chasing the dragon", forgetting to give enough time and dedication to do the work in integrating what they learned at these workshops back into their daily lives.

Making the Shift

Regardless of which group we are more similar to, we go through the regular motions of life, until something major happens. This can be:

- **Unpleasant**: We broke up with a long-standing partner or we got divorced, we lose someone we love to death, we lose our jobs suddenly, we got struck by a natural disaster, we or someone dear to us got diagnosed with a major illness, etc., or
- **Pleasant:** We won a lottery or a gold medal, we met the love of our life, we won a championship we trained so hard for, we got engaged or married because we wanted to, we fell pregnant after trying for years, we landed a lucrative contract we worked painstakingly for, etc.

Or simply, through the course of life, we wake up one day and feel within every inch of our being that enough is enough (enough of being constantly angry/feeling helpless or sorry for myself/obliging to others etc.), or with a sense that, this is not good enough for me, and...

We commit to shift.

We then go through a range of emotions (or not, depending on how we cope).

We do things to feel better or even to be better. We enter an in-between period, a space where we have moved away from the old but not quite arriving at the new place yet, and where going back to the old is neither viable nor desirable.

We may become restless, impatient, confused, snappy or plain 'blah'.

The Invisible Opportunity

But, there is another face to this Stuck State. I like to call it the Invisible Opportunity.

I'm certain we are familiar with the simile of a glass half empty or half full, where the difference lies in the perspective taken.

What's more important however, is the acknowledgement that only when a glass of water is emptied can it be filled with fresh water.

Similarly, when you are afraid but don't know that you are afraid, or when you know something needs to change but don't know what, where, why or how to effect that change, these are the times when there is an invisible opportunity to discover something new to learn about and grow from.

> *This requires us to begin by momentarily emptying ourselves of what we think we know from our past experience.*

I think it is crucial for us to get to know this period fully in its own right; how a Stuck State with an invisible opportunity feels, and experience it in full.

The crucial point and the big reason for this is that it is not the speed with which one moves from Stuck State to unstuck that marks its success, but the quality of the movement from the Stuck State.

Each one of us, at every phase of our lives, will experience this differently.

Therefore, it is important that we do not rush to move things along or make sense of things in the head or fix things. Allowing for personal space and rest will enable and support a more thorough processing of deep personal change.

The quality of the movement taking place during a significant personal change is strongly influenced by the quality of personal space and rest we can allow.

The more open and safely held the space is, the more restful we can be, i.e. the better the quality of personal space and rest, the better the movement will be.

Moving Well

When we are moving well from a Stuck State, our Whole Capacity is getting mobilised, and we begin to receive and digest 'new data'.

Some common signs of this are: we start to "see" some things that we did not see before, ideas or actions that we once valued lose their stronghold, and we are quite happy to do what we might never have even considered to do before.

The crucial point is not the speed with which we move from Stuck State to unstuck but the quality of the movement.

My most closely held personal example of this was when I experienced my very first systemic constellation.

I had brought an issue for light to be casted upon. For as long as I could remember, I had lived with underlying anxiety.

I was constantly feeling as if life is coming to an end for me and I had to do everything I wanted to do, yesterday. I had a need to keep moving, and this surfaced in the form of needing to move from place to place, relationship to relationship, job to job, idea to idea, project to project… as if, if I didn't, my life would be so insignificant that I would be insignificant and disappear.

I was tired of operating in this state, and I knew that something had to shift because I was definitely not well and happy with the status quo.

If you are not familiar with systemic constellations, the process is a trans-generational, phenomenological, therapeutic intervention with roots in family systems therapy, existential-phenomenology, and the ancestor appreciation of the South African Zulus.

A constellation can serve as an illuminating adjunct process within a conventional course of psychotherapy.

While it is rooted in the psychotherapeutic tradition, the method is distinguished from conventional psychotherapy in that the client hardly speaks, and its primary aim is to identify and release deep patterns embedded within the client system, rather than to extensively explore verbalised narrative, cognitive or emotional content.

Here is what unfolded for me over three days at the first ever constellations workshop I attended.

I brought an issue to the room. The issue was one of the many symptoms of life challenges that I was processing, i.e. generalised low-grade anxiety. I chose representatives of parts of my system to take their place vis-à-vis each other.

Through the dynamics at play, first, I saw that I had stood in a particular place in my family of origin that I then replicated in every other aspect of my life. I was the mediator, the harmoniser, the obedient, the quiet, the absorber, the carer, the parent, the triangulated...

Next, I realised that the reason I had zero desire to have my own children up until that point was because I had taken on the pains of my mother and all the feminine line she carried in her, as if they were mine.

I had identified with all the women in my family through my grandmothers and my mother, and lived my life the way I imagined my mother would have wanted to if she were to live her life all over again.

I believed that my mother would choose to be out working and enjoying a successful career instead of staying home to look after the house and children, that she would choose not to have any children and that she would have left her marriage.

The realisation broke me and restored me at the same time. I had lived my life feeling like some sort of a warrior; I had wanted the pain of all the women in my family line to stop with me.

I felt strong and powerful and I thought I was complete and whole. But there was a brittleness in that superficial strength, power and wholeness.

I did not realise that I had rejected my feminine part and had come to identify with my masculine part as the safer, more reliable and rewarding one for me.

Another version of this story was that I lived my life as if I did not value it enough to want to pass it on.

I cried so much in the three days and for the first time in my life after the workshop, I experienced a day without anxiety.

I was sitting on the train when I clocked total silence within, zero anxiety, zero worries, zero planning. I was still journaling when I realised that this experience was so alien to me that I started to look for things to be anxious about.

That was when I caught myself. And with that, I received a new choice I could exercise. I realised how much I had identified anxiety as part of who I am that I did not know how to live without it. I thought to myself, "Ok, I know all these now, so what do I do?"

I asked the facilitator, who later became one of my teachers when I studied systemic constellations, "What do I do with all these realisations?"

Her answer was simple, "Nothing. For now, just sit with it. You will do what you need to do, in time."

Another day passed. Indeed, I woke up feeling different. The switch of my non-desire to have my own children flicked, as if by magic. It was unexpected and surprising and I found it very hard to believe.

I gave it time and when months later, the desire to be a mother did not fade, I knew that my core light, my own truth, had shone through.

For the first time in my life, I experienced a day without anxiety.

Whilst it took an overnight flick of the magic switch to move from never wanting to have my own child to being broody, it took me awhile to make sense of what happened such that I could share it in a practical way.

As I began to see new aspects of who I am, aspects that I did not yet know I would have the capacity for, my work was to welcome and invite them in, get to know them, and give them space and nurturing to blossom.

This is crucial. If there is no space for nurturing the new aspect, no caring for the soil where this fresh sprout was peeking its head out, it will die, and we will be left with the barrenness we knew before.

The tendered soil and nurturing environment transforms the sprout of potential, the invisible opportunity, with new insight, into fresh possibility.

Without the right holding environment, the sprout of potential cannot grow into its optimal state of being. The quality of nurturing is so important in enabling a good movement forward.

Improving the Quality

So how do we go about improving the quality of this movement?

Simply put, through patience and with practice, ideally working with someone you trust.

Through patience and with practice, we can signpost crucial moments and points of change, and move through them more consciously in our own way.

We learn to use the information we have and hold from our life and trust our inner voice. Marking movements by signposting helps us in navigating growth inflections in life.

This is what our forefathers have done through ancient practices in rites of passage.

Many of us have lost touch with these practices although in some communities, some of them do take place in traditional ceremonies, such as when a girl gets her first period.

We can use totems or symbols and apply the principles of rites of passage to support the movement forward from the Stuck State. Cultivating an appreciation for such symbolisms that rites of passage mark can serve as a nourishing container for a person growing through the course of life.

There is an exercise that I like because of its sheer simplicity. It involves charting one's life from birth up to this point in time, marking high points and low points, and peeling off the layers of stories, reasoning, beliefs and emotions to discover the raw feelings that lay beneath.

Specific "rituals" can then be designed and followed through to mark significant life stages and changes that were never fully honoured before.

Some stages could be neutral, some painfully charged with emotions, while some very fondly attaching. People are often pleasantly surprised to discover their many identities, that they were all of them, all of them in the past, present and future.

It is very freeing to learn that one can let them all be there in an inspiring way and not have them running or ruling or even "ruining" lives.

With proper guidance and facilitation as well as self-reflection, this exercise can be very powerful not just to support the quality of movement, but to help one in releasing the pains of old wounds in the psyche.

The Finishing Line?

It is important for me to state at this juncture that I believe there is no finish line in the journey of personal growth.

I easily acknowledged this very early on in my development work. But the deeper realisation of what it truly meant only came some time after.

I thought I was ambivalent about that statement in that I did not have any strong feelings. It existed simply as a conclusion I had arrived at until I started to unpack the belief and suspended logic and reasoning that my feelings became apparent.

I noticed feelings of tiredness and helplessness and then, a little later on, I felt relief and empowerment. I did not know why but it did not feel important for me then to know why.

Some more years later, in inquiring into why some experiences leave impressions strong enough to propel individuals to take different courses of action, I learned about inner movement and what it means to be deeply moved or motivated.

There is a different quality to this movement from if we were to compare it to the excitement that comes from discovering our passion and then pursuing it.

The inner movement is more subtle and less tangible in terms of overt action, and it feels more like a resolution to be different first, before the doing. I started calling this Sub-movement, short for Subtle Movement.

When we expand our capacity to recognise invisible opportunities, we enjoy an improved quality of life.

This marks the true beginning of becoming unstuck. It is the beginning of seeing an invisible opportunity. This Sub-movement greatly influences the quality of the outer movement.

The invisible opportunity of the belief "there is no finish line in the journey of personal growth" is that life continues to grow in many interesting dimensions even as we age and believe that there is no more learning to be had.

The work here is to learn to recognise and appreciate the invisible opportunity when we move from the Stuck State.

When we expand our capacity to recognise invisible opportunities, we not only move through the Stuck State more effectively, we enjoy an improved quality of life and slow down the decay of our physical bodies.

We then keep growing our Whole Capacity.

It's a vicious cycle. It is therefore so important to support this movement and do all we can to ensure efficient navigation, particularly when this "do all we can" is not actually the overt doing of anything.

Navigation suffers when a life-changing event takes place as an unwelcome surprise or it happens too suddenly, when too many changes are happening at the same time, when past changes never fully completed, or when no proper time was invested to reflect and integrate for personal growth.

Having enough support is crucial. Recognising this and being able to draw support is likely to make the biggest difference.

Reflection Points

What do you feel Stuck about or wish to get unstuck?

What views or beliefs are you particularly attached to?

Do they explain or justify your Stuck State? Do they free you, or hold you back?

Can you open your mind up and allow space in your heart to design more helpful beliefs?

What life-enhancing outcomes and possibilities will you shape for yourself?

WAY #2: GETTING TO KNOW YOUR IDENTITIES

Some years ago… as I was starting to develop the ideas for this book… I shared a curry in London with an old friend.

I met Greg, who is male, white and British, through an Organisation Development programme I was participating in. We were reuniting in London to share an Indian meal together.

The food, decor and service at the restaurant were authentically Indian and I felt very much in the right place.

The mix of spices from India with local ingredients, cooked to perfection and served in small copper-looking pots, hit the precise notes for us to engage in a conversation about Identity, one of the elements to Whole Capacity.

Greg left his marriage of 10 years with his high-school sweetheart whom he had known for 10 years prior to getting married. Together they have two daughters.

His reason seemed simple enough; remaining in that marriage would have not allowed him to live one of his core identities.

Greg discovered in his teens that he was interested in men. In these moments he would catch himself and judge his thoughts, "This is not normal, not natural".

His feelings of guilt were so big that he repressed this for many years without even daring to think about it.

In the years that followed, he revisited and reconnected with these thoughts and feelings, and over time, came to recognise that this was something that really mattered to him.

The social convention, cultural norms and broad belief that heterosexuality is "the right" and "only normal way", clearly tried to force this square peg into a round hole.

The impact was so pronounced that despite that prominent experience, he managed to convince himself that he was bisexual and could have a faithful loving relationship with a woman... enough to marry and start a family with her.

Greg spoke with real pain as he recalled the difficulty of coming to the decision that would impact three important women he loves dearly.

The road to allowing one of his identities that is core to come to the foreground, to be owned and lived, can be too painful for some.

It takes enormous awareness, courage and personal conviction, as well as some semblance of support mechanism, for those whose life experience had blown their blinkers into ether, to actually make that step change.

In the case of Greg, his sexual identity is a big part of his overall Identity, and therefore according to him, it felt too significant for him to disregard this core identity any longer than he already had.

This is why we need to look deeply into our Identity.

Always Evolving

As decent human beings, we are constantly evolving. Getting to know our Identity enables us to:
- Expand our range of being.
- Live more freely and joyfully with less judgment, grounded in our own essence and sense of purpose.
- Connect with others in that way.
- Learn to take ourselves less seriously so we can keep remembering all of who we are.
- Bring forth bravery and courage to contribute to the beauty of our world.
- Live interdependently, co-creatively, and leave a legacy.

Much of what we do is driven by our identities, and in order for us to have a better idea of what drives us, what holds us back and what we are perpetuating on a day-to-day basis, we need to get to know our identities.

Some of these identities are tucked away from our own consciousness, and only show up in times of crisis or when our psyche is ready to deal with it.

It definitely pays to be curious about ourselves and nurture a level of readiness so that when any unfamiliar identities reveal themselves, we are better-equipped to welcome and integrate them.

From the stories people have shared and my conversations with experienced human development practitioners, inquiries into Identity have helped people deepen the connection with themselves, and through this, they learn to live with a greater sense of purpose and cooperation.

Many have broken away from unhelpful patterns of behaviour and relationships and past conditioning to actively co-create a different future.

Others report discovering and reconnecting with their natural powers and talent, accessing them to serve oneself well and present a gift to humanity. Some say that they developed allies with all their relations, whether known, seen or felt, internal or external, and as a result, began to feel supported in life, and live life without feeling alone.

In order for us to have a better idea of what drives us and what holds us back, we need to get to know our identities.

I shared in the preface about the experience of "dying" as I lived the darkest period of my life going through my divorce, moving away from my motherland and changing career.

While, for some, a divorce is a challenging but not a life-changing experience, my personal experience was profound because the decision I made challenged all of what I believed I was, up to that point in time.

Amongst others, I believed that:
- I ought to marry the one man who is trustworthy, smart and dependable.
- I must remain with this one man "in sickness and in health, till death do us part".
- To get a divorce is to concede failure and embarrass my family.
- To leave a man who is emotionally unwell is an irresponsible and shamefully selfish act.

- To leave a marriage and motherland simultaneously is self-centred, not filial and a cause of pain, etc.

Exposing Beliefs

When those beliefs got exposed, I did not know what to do with myself.
- Who was I supposed to marry?
- Why should I even be married?
- What kind of a woman am I?
- What kind of a daughter am I?
- What kind of a person am I?
- Am I not the kind and loving one who becomes a reason for a man to heal?
- Am I not the successful and ambitious woman with a generous heart of gold?
- How can I even be happy with my decision when others are hurting from it?

Experiencing my divorce led me to working with a wise elder, an 80-year-old Gestalt therapist, and together we began to discover and recover, piece by piece, core parts of me. I realised that most of who I knew myself to be, the identities that stood in the foreground, had been defined by others.

The new identities I was coming to terms with – the divorced, irresponsible, not filial, betrayer – were also defined by others.

I rejected the new while being attached to the old (successful, responsible, filial, and trustworthy) which I thought and believed had come from my own aspirations.

The whole senses an imbalance and this fuels its own attempt at becoming whole again.

I did not think that it was my *attachment* to what I identified with, instead of the values themselves, which was causing most of the pain.

Ironically, those judgments were not entirely mine either.

Because I had such a strong attachment to being identified as successful, responsible, filial and trustworthy, and because it impacts my sense of belonging to my family of origin, the opposing forces came on just as strongly.

Systems seek to balance; the Whole senses an imbalance and this fuels its own attempt at becoming Whole again. My system is trying to self-heal but I was not allowing it to.

Four Points of Identity

This is why it is important to understand these four points on Identity:

1. We are born into some and we acquire others as we change and grow.
2. The birth of new ones change the way the pre-existing ones live.
3. Rejecting or attaching to any one Identity creates an imbalance to the whole.
4. This energetic imbalance will fuel the whole to seek balance.

In my current life, I was born into my ethnicity and nationality, and I birthed into a daughter and sister.

As I grew in life, I welcomed more role-related identities - friend, student, writer, colleague, consultant, coach, wife, catalyst, mother, leader.

Then I committed to even more - vegetarian, raw organic whole foods fan, vegan, vehicle for transformation. And I identified with concepts like being a life-long learner, practising kindness and empathy, being open and honest, being trustworthy and loving.

Birth of New Identities

When new identities are birthed, as in the case of becoming a mother for example, how I am as a wife changes.

If I am attached to how I must remain as the kind of wife I was before baby arrived, I expend most of my energy to be the wife I was and I am unable to fully welcome the becoming of a mother.

The same goes the other way round. If I rejected becoming a mother, I am unable to fully welcome the mother that is just born.

An energetic system will always seek to be in balance.

Therefore, when one is attaching or rejecting, the energy is concentrated on one part at the expense of another.

The unfortunate thing is that for some, the expense shows up in the form of unhealthy patterns of behaviour and relationships, depression, and even physical ailments.

Sometimes we may be tempted to "disown" the identities that we think are not our identities of choice.

However, the moment we allow the "new identity" to arrive, to fully come to the foreground and be truly seen, we acknowledge it as a part of us worth seeing, and our whole system receives the honour it is given and "calms down".

An inner movement starts to take place and when this happens, love can flow, energy can flow, and we grow.

In times of personal crisis, I often encountered people ultimately arriving at the questions, "who am I?" and "why am I here?"

Similarly, virtually everyone who gets into deep personal development work, whether self-initiated or as part of an organisation's leadership development initiatives, often reach a point where they have to deal with such an identity crisis at some point.

Sometimes we may be tempted to "disown" the identities that we think are not our identities of choice, identities that don't really feel like who we are or who we want to be.

However, the very act of rejecting… even if these identities were "borrowed" or have passed their expiry date of being helpful… triggers an opposing force because they all have a place in the psyche.

This is why, when we hold an expanded perspective of our whole being, we will have space for all parts of ourselves to be included and belong, without judgment.

Defining Identity

I have deliberately not defined Identity up to this point because I wanted to lay the context.

The word Identity has its roots in 16th century Latin idem, which means same, and from late Latin *identitas*, which means having the quality of being identical.

> ***Identity, in short, is that which is you... that which makes you and is also you.***

Your identities, i.e. the many aspects of you that make up all that you are, I refer to as Identity.

I won't get into a detailed analysis and all the psycho-social theories of Identity, but I will share what I found through my work that stood out as profound and challenging, interesting and useful, and dissect the Identity element using some basic points and perspectives as frames.

At this point, I wish to offer two perspectives on Identity:

1. **Our identities are largely conditioned:** Our identities are formed from the moment of conception (our consciousness even before that).

    They are shaped and influenced by various interacting systems, biological, familial and socio-cultural.

    Therefore, there arise many aspects to a person – the physical body, tribal or national heritage, beliefs, behaviours, thoughts, feelings, emotions etc.

    Some of these aspects we embrace, some we ignore, reject or crave for, and some are yet to be discovered.

In this regard, we can say that most, if not all, identities are conditioned.

2. **Our identities are largely relational:** Who we are, is relational – we cannot be like this if there is nothing like that; we cannot be something without anything else to exist against.

    Every aspect of us exists in relation to something, be it internal within ourselves or external with others.

    So in this sense, when we reject one Identity, whether ours or someone else's, we are also rejecting a part of ourselves, whether we like it or not.

    Our feelings act as an enormous compass that guide us towards what we see in others as well as ourselves.

    This is precious because what we cannot see, we cannot include, and what we exclude cannot inform our actions.

This begs other questions like:
- How do all my identities relate with each other?
- Are they in harmony?
- If they are not, am I at risk of denying any one or splitting off my identities or compartmentalising the different aspects of myself to unhealthy extremes that may well lead to pent up emotions and diseases?
- Why are some of my identities more important, i.e. why are they in the foreground?
- What makes me push some of my identities to the background?

- Do we know which identities need to be nurtured or nursed, and what to do about them?

Safe Space

Greg and I were fortunate in that we found our web of trust, people who walked with us through the crisis while holding a safe space for us to digest and process our experiences.

We have made it our life mission to walk with others facing life-work-relationship challenges and together we grow humanity, starting with ourselves.

Parking all theories, models and hypothesis for a moment, we know from the depths of our whole being as human development catalysts, that engendering a sense of safety is crucial to co-creating optimal conditions for human growth.

Otherwise, whilst people can definitely learn something from any life experience, without an effective holding environment, they may not grow much from that learning.

In the following chapters, we will look into this thing called holding environment. Suffice to say, when we consciously explore Identity in order to deepen our own understanding of who we are, whether this is through a personalised or off-the-shelf intervention, facilitated or otherwise, we enter into a beautiful dimension where anything is possible.

The ability to simplify and focus leads to clarity so that we can receive an intimate appreciation of oneself and access infinite possibilities.

Reflection Points

Have you ever experienced the coming in of a new Identity – getting married, being a new mum, getting divorced, being a new manager, receiving an award, becoming an overnight celebrity, or even recalling a past life? What happened to you?

Have you ever rejected, repressed or suppressed a part of you – being of a particular religion, race, gender, birth order, sexual preference etc.? What did you sacrifice? What was the price you paid for giving up that part of you?

Have you ever asked yourself at a particular point in time, "Who is Here, Right Now? Who is here right now, with in, in you and as you?"

You can perform an Identity Exercise.

Cut a circle out of a blank sheet of paper. Grab a few coloured pens. Get into your body before you begin. I typically close my eyes and practice mindful breathing for 30-60 seconds, or if you have five minutes, that's even better. During this time, observe thoughts and inner voices arising. Just notice, judgments, cynicism, doubts, positive and negative feelings. Then begin.

Ask yourself, "Who Is Here, Right Now?" Then draw and place everything and everyone that come up for you. Use your coloured pens. Afterwards, reflect on these questions and journal:

- *What have I excluded here?*
- *Who have I excluded?*
- *What am I hiding?*
- *What am I pretending to be?*
- *What am I afraid of?*

WAY #3: GETTING IN THE FLOW OF YOUR TRUE NATURE

Many people I meet are very attached to one particular version of who they are and the possibilities for alternative expressions of their identity and nature… perhaps healthier, happier, freer versions… are blocked away.

If we realise that we are renewing our cells every single day… that what we energetically focus on and surround ourselves in can influence our being and becoming… then in effect, we can meet the highest version of ourselves.

That's the one that embodies full optimal living, the one that lives our Whole Capacity more and more often, so that it becomes our dominant nature.

When this happens, we not only have the positive impact that we desire on ourselves and others, we begin to experience life in its richest yet simplest of ways.

The experience of living in love, beauty, joy, purpose, passion, a sense of mission or calling, contentment, positivity, optimal health and abundance, is a given.

We are living our Whole Capacity.

I have worked with many individuals making career and life changes. Some believe that moving from one country or company to another is the key to resolution.

Others choose to bring forth an emerging identity while remaining in the same environment.

In both cases, there might be very little appreciation for the concept of an emerging identity calling out for a change, and a strong existing identity that needs to move to the background and make space for the new.

The Third Entity

This is why it is so important to consider the third entity, which I call Nature.

In the interaction between identities and the context that the identities find themselves in and dancing with, a third entity is born.

> *If we realise that we are renewing our cells every single day, then in effect, we can meet the highest version of ourselves.*

It is born of the dance and is also the dance. Together, the identity, context and nature make for a holding environment.

This holding environment receives information external to it, and sends information back out.

This idea casts some light that can support shifting identities. If there is a grasp of the concept that this dance exists and is a very real entity in its own right, the process of transformation leading to growth, or the sustained movement from Stuck to Unstuck, can be co-designed, co-created, co-nurtured, and co-supported, all the way in attuning with each other.

- When all components are attuned to each other, the holding environment is in **harmony**.
- When they are in the process of attuning, the holding environment is in what is referred to here as the **Perfect Storm**.

It can be described as Perfect because it is seeking optimal wholeness and it can be described as a Storm because like a storm, it is a resulting process that seems chaotic, yet necessary and 'cleansing'.

The Perfect Storm

Consider this for a moment. Storms form in response to an extreme difference in air pressure, driven by the movement of cold and warm air.

This combination of opposing forces creates winds and results in the formation of storm clouds, such as the cumulonimbus.

Eventually either the cold or warm air dissipates, and equilibrium becomes re-established and calm, less-windy weather prevails.

The atmosphere moves toward equilibrium, therefore when low pressure develops, air pours in to fill it quite like having water rush out from a bathtub full of water when the plug is pulled. The water from the tub rushes in to fill the hole in the drain.

In the atmosphere, rather than the air draining 'down', it drains 'up' towards the less dense environment of the upper atmosphere.

Air moves from areas of relatively high pressure towards areas of relative low pressure to create equilibrium. The greater the pressure difference, the stronger the wind.

Analogous to that, the attuning process in the holding environment, i.e. the Perfect Storm, is more chaotic when either one of the three entities are significantly in need of rebalancing.

> ***The perfection in these storms lies in the way that it is driven towards bringing to surface what needs to be addressed.***

The Perfect Storm determines which genetic code gets switched on or off, what neural pathways need re-patterning, and it wakes us up to our innate capability of birthing and rebirthing ourselves, moment by moment.

It can also be known as interdependent co-arising. This is our Nature.

Being afraid of the Perfect Storm may not be helpful because the storm is both necessary and natural.

It is in our Nature to re-pattern through seeming chaos, providing we engage the necessary supportive forces and holding processes, and keep getting out of our own way.

There are vital ways to work with this so that we can let Nature do its thing and allow our life energy to flow in health.

A short and simple example I will share here again, is the time when I left my first marriage and moved to London.

Moving to London gave me the space to examine my context (family expectations and tradition), and my Identity (the type of wife and daughter I wanted to be known as), in order to work on my nature, i.e. the dance between my emerging identity (perhaps a Bohemian divorcee) and my emerging context (the new texture in which I experience my family expectations and tradition), by engaging the vital supportive conditions, so that I can evolve.

When I could immerse in my Nature, my emerging identity and context were given full permission to be born.

The Perfect Storm wakes us up to our innate capability of rebirthing ourselves, moment by moment.

Through engaging the necessary supportive forces and holding processes, I was able to get out of my way often enough such that the quality of my inner movement through the Stuck-Unstuck State is high.

This paved the path for my optimal Nature to come to its fullest expression. It was a very stormy period of my life, but it was the Perfect Storm.

The Concept of Nature

According to Wikipedia, the word nature is derived from the Latin word *natura*, or "essential qualities, innate disposition", and in ancient times, literally meant "birth".

Natura was a Latin translation of the Greek word physis, which originally related to the intrinsic characteristics that plants, animals, and other features of the world develop of their own accord.

The concept of Nature as a whole, the physical universe, is one of several expansions of the original notion.

Today, "nature" often refers to geology and wildlife. It is often taken to mean the "natural environment" or wilderness–wild animals, rocks, forest, beaches, and in general those things that have not been substantially altered by human intervention, or which persist despite human intervention.

How we are formed at conception, the energetic data coded in every cell before and after the foetus forms, and how we grow from inside the womb up to the present moment brings about our very first Nature.

The environment in which our born identities live and interact with then influences the blossoming of our Nature.

Learning about our Nature helps us to live with flow and authenticity.

Understanding this, we become more aware of what shapes the very first Nature of all human beings, what helps or hinders the blossoming of our Nature, and what we can do about it on a practical level to keep evolving.

- It helps us know how we dance in life, and this in turn can help us claim our own power while empowering others.
- It helps us live with more bravery and vulnerability than ever, and with greater consciousness of our impact on humanity so we can better support each other in living well, together.

Following Nature

I can never forget the day I got to know Laurence like I never did before.

Laurence was one of my favourite lunch buddies in London because of the very, very interesting conversations we would have.

He is sensitive, present and perceptive, and had many stories to share from all his travelling, research, filming and broadcasting projects. At the time of writing, Laurence was heading up the research and campaigns arm of a UK charity.

One day, I asked him to tell me about some experiences that led to profound growth and how the process unfolded. He shared a few, two of which particularly stood out.

At 11, Laurence decided he wasn't going to follow his parents' religion. He told his father and the Rabbi that he was not going to be an Orthodox Jew.

He thought that he was simply stating the obvious because it didn't make sense for him since he didn't believe in God (the way he was taught about it).

However, the reaction he got from these prominent figures of authority was surprising to the boy and very frightening. He felt at odds with his family and he turned against his father.

Learning about our Nature helps us to live with flow and authenticity.

Soon, he fell out with his schoolmates and got into a lot of fighting. It was a tough time and although he managed to cope quite well, he was deeply affected by this dark period and the voices of judgment would keep replaying in times of vulnerability. He says:

> *"I wasn't really aware of it (the voices of judgment) coming in and out. My mind seems to remember only the pattern, not the content."*

By 21, Laurence was working for one of the best record companies in the world. He adds:

> *"I was fortunate to earn lots of money, but unfortunate to not know what to do in life. I made the classic mistake of thinking, 'I can handle it.'"*

Laurence's exploration with drugs had grown from curiosity of the varieties of drugs and the enjoyment of mind-expanding experiences, to progressively enter into a deadly addiction. He comments:

> *"Escapism can be therapeutic, but if not careful, it can turn destructive. I took it too far. I became physically addicted to Class A drugs. It seemed like I found the answer to all my problems but that answer soon became the problem."*

Laurence sold his shares in the company and received a seven-figure sum. He spent years partying and taking drugs, and later on, ended up just taking drugs. He added:

> *"It was a slow, steady decline, until my survival instinct kicked in. I had to dig myself out of the hole, otherwise I would die. Unfortunately, none of the programmes in the detox centres worked. I was quite resistant to change. In the end, I did it myself. I spent three months in Tunisia getting healthy."*

The trigger was his wife's insistence and his agreement to start counselling. He comments:

> *"My therapist said that under normal circumstances, I would have to be clean before therapy began, but he could see that I had a real problem, and he said that he would help work with me until I could get to a point where I'd get clean.*
> *That really, really helped. I thought my problem was taking too much drugs, but actually that was just the symptom of a very troubled mind, in all its order, structure, patterns and conditioning. I was tangled up. I wasn't able to see clearly. I had lost my ability to function properly."*

Entanglement

Through my work and personal inquiry, I found that one of the most common challenges to living our Whole Capacity is entanglement.

Entanglement happen when one's identities become unhealthily bonded to other significant persons' identities.

Our Nature is compromised. These bonds then exert powerful influences in the individual's own system, increasing tensions in the system, and eventually lead to "sickness".

Highly sensitive and empathic individuals struggle with this much more since they are more likely to find it difficult to implement clear boundaries between where they finish and where others begin.

They therefore more easily succumb to entanglement than less sensitive individuals. Such is the price paid for the gift of empathy.

Laurence spent years getting into the 'dark dungeon' and more years coming out of it.

He found his way through understanding his Nature (to resist impositions and authority), and living through the Perfect Storm. His therapist, his wife, his intellect, his inner light, his emerging identity as a clean, clear-headed, disentangled man and aspiring father who serves mankind, all held him as he birthed this emerging identity.

He says, "I've had to find out for myself what's the best way to live, mostly by making mistakes. I was confronted with a great necessity to change. I continue to learn and hopefully develop the capacity to hold and recognise my experience, my environment and myself, in parallel.

Living life is like tending the garden, where learning can seem painstakingly slow, and often frustrated by many surprises, until sudden insight and breakthrough arrive.

The more experiences I have, the more able I grow to be in joining many perspectives together to make the connections quicker, and arrive at the bigger picture."

Live Your Whole Capacity

Living life is like tending the garden, where learning can seem painstakingly slow.

When I first started learning about "hidden dynamics" in my organisational work, it gave me a mapping framework and helped me understand why I received so much positive feedback about my political awareness.

It helped me learn how I can hone this capacity in a way that allows me to effect change more easily and synthesise it into a shareable form. I also improved my knowledge about my biases; what tends to fall into my blind spot and the pattern of occurrences when I misread.

It wasn't until I studied systemic constellations that I developed a fuller appreciation for the mechanics behind the invisible dance forces.

Through the shared client-colleague space (I often experience clients as colleagues whenever we consciously engage in systemic work), I experienced profoundly the natural ability for systems to self-organise, seek balance, and self-heal, providing the elements dancing together are broadly healthy and not entangled.

Re-membering, i.e. collecting our Nature back into us as a valid and important member of our whole system is essential.

The better we get at sensing the dance between the entities, the better we get at supporting our own growth, the better we will flow in life.

> **Reflection Points**
>
> *When you experienced a welcome or a rejection of an Identity, what were the circumstances surrounding you then?*
>
> *What did the major life changes mean for you at the deepest level; what did you feel?*
>
> *How did you respond? If you could turn back time, how would you have responded instead?*
>
> *How have you experienced the change?*

WAY #4: KEEP LIVING MORE CONSCIOUSLY

During a Perfect Storm of the type discussed in the previous chapter, we may find our blinkers being blown away and we start to experience a fresh take at life.

We find it different as compared to how we knew it before, as if we had been living half-blind in the past.

When the storm passes, often there is a feeling of relief and gratitude, like we have been given a second chance at life. This could then be followed by a sense of wonder as to what the future may hold.

Increasing Happiness

Mark is the leader of a movement to increase happiness in the world. I was part of that movement and felt drawn to Mark by virtue of the glimmer in his eyes which spoke of his ability to see deeply, and his open gestures had a certain ease which seemed to suggest that he had made a number of recent, conscious choices in his life.

Over a vegan sandwich lunch in a park near his office, Mark gave me a glimpse into his past, which confirmed my hunch.

I have spoken to many people who shared a similar pattern - middle class family, studied hard, got a respected job, worked hard, made good money, and then experienced a breakdown of sorts which led them to question why they were doing what they were doing, and what was it that they wanted to be doing instead.

Mark's version of the story was interesting in that he already had a wide exposure to many industries coming from a Big 4 consulting background, but still decided to do an MBA in a bid to find his path, when Love called.

He became curious about human psychology in general, and in one of his elective courses, he was assigned a Jungian therapist to work with for a year. Says Mark:

> *"I was interested to experience it even though when we began, I didn't think I had any pressing issue. My back pain, which I learned was caused by stress, had disappeared by then, and I felt well.*
> *But I came out of these sessions progressively realising that I was more messed up than I thought I was, in a good way! It gave me chance to grow deeply, to be the best that I can be.*
> *I became increasingly curious and developed a passion for learning about how we all function as human beings, and how we can influence social policy to improve our lives.*
> *Martin Seligman and Neil Crofts were my big influencers at that time. I got clearer about how I wanted to apply myself and began to develop meta-cognition, i.e. clocking that I'm angry when I'm feeling angry, and therefore being able to make new choices for response."*

When his first child arrived, Mark experienced another big catalyst for change. His home life had completely changed and he was tired and frustrated at the office.

He worked with a coach who had a way for working with the subconscious, and he began to see that his work-life balance issue was not about the organisation he was serving, but about him… his inability to say "No" plus his obsession with wanting to please.

He also noticed his instinct to praise his child, and he began to recognise at the same time, how praise had impacted him, in an unbalanced way, growing up. Mark comments:

> *"Growing up with praise on the results I got trained me to seek praise as a form of validation. I was only satisfied when I did something that people liked or valued. I wasn't happy or at ease just being me.*
> *Of course, praise helped me to excel academically and land good jobs, but it made me somewhat neurotic, imbalanced and without peace.*
> *With my children today, I try to focus on praising the effort rather than the result. I guess I'm a recovering people pleaser!"*

Mark observed that so many organisations are "imbalanced" and have "massive blind spots" that obstruct them from becoming healthily balanced.

Practically all major blue-chip companies value "left-brain skills" and use consulting firms that are also heavily left-brained, for advice.

They attract and retain left-brained oriented staff and penalise the more right-brain oriented ones, running the risk of producing "role models for obsession rather than balance."

Mark was able to make these observations when his blinkers were blown away, through shifting of Identities and a reclaiming of his Nature as he lived through his Perfect Storms - career change and becoming a parent.

He lives his life more consciously than before, as he examined how he came to his decisions in the past, before his stormy periods, versus how he is making decisions in the aftermath.

> *Once we cross the invisible line between our last and our current level of consciousness, there is no way to turn back.*

We cannot un-see what is already seen. The beauty of this is the gift of experiencing life with newfound aliveness, whether the feelings that come up are pleasant or unpleasant.

The gifts that could come are the chipping away of old habits or patterns that no longer serve us, the establishing of clearer boundaries between our co-existing identities and those of others, and living our best in every single new breath we take.

We can keep learning how to live from a happier, healthier place.

Conscious living could be triggered spontaneously as a result of going through life's natural courses. But to enable a progressive continuation of conscious living requires effort on our part to make decisions in that direction, through exercising alternative choices.

When we choose to live consciously, we release and manifest our creativity and allow flow to carry us.

When we choose to live consciously, we release and manifest our creativity and allow flow to carry us.

The more we live consciously and give ourselves space, the more we allow a healthier rhythm to carry many of our possibilities into form. The question then becomes:

- How can we open up space in our lives such that we enable optimal flow and manifestation?
- How can we make this part of our everyday living?

Meditation

Many of us know that when done well, meditation and yoga undeniably teach us about this thing called space through direct experience.

The idea is that over time, with regular practice, our mind and body are rewired and reshaped in a way that enables us to experience space more often as we go about our daily activities.

There is no denying however, that the space we experience during formal practice, whereby time is set aside for dedicated practice in a safe and contained environment, separate from our regular lives, is indeed rather different compared to finding or making space in all the buzz as we move through in the course of life.

Before my daughter was born, I regularly practiced formal meditation and yoga, and was a loyal fan of retreats that ran for more than a week.

The longer retreats allowed me to inquire deeply and learn about myself through active observation amidst the simplest of activities. In doing so, it gave my body and mind a "full holiday".

I often returned to my regular world fully resourced; recharged energetically, inspired by the ideas and insights that have emerged for me, and feeling capable of coping with anything that life was to throw at me.

Moving from monastic-style living where the way of life as exemplified at retreats is ring-fenced from income-generating and relationship-driven activities, back to active participation in lay worldly affairs, did not make it easy for me to maintain the results of a retreat for long.

I would try harder at being more mindful and fitting in formal practice whenever I could, and was mildly successful, but very soon, the expanded capacity earned from a retreat would fade away with my depleting energy. And I would yearn for another retreat to recharge my batteries.

Sharpening

At the time, I had started working on sharpening myself as an instrument of change within my capacity as an organisation development consultant.

I found a mentor, someone who embodied that capacity in the field of organisation development, and who had done significant amounts of personal work to develop that capacity.

Through his experience, I learned and became curious about the role that breathwork and systemic constellations could play in both personal and organisation growth.

I participated in my first breathwork retreat in California with a tinge of nervousness and extremely high hopes for breakthrough results. I was somewhat disappointed that nothing extraordinary happened, but I returned with one ordinary nugget that would be so precious for me in time to come.

I learned about the importance of growing my personal web of support. By simply holding that in my mind, the design and development of a personal holding structure began to unfold for me.

Web of Support

The breathwork in and of itself, is a mind-expanding experience.

However, through the space in the entire retreat, I experienced the holding structure that was enacted and I mapped it out to realise what made the learning experience and growth more sustainable for me than it otherwise would have been.

I found myself spontaneously considering, who are my "elders", who are my "sisters", where do I feel strong and what about those places that nourished me, how was I dialoguing and with whom, what have I censored and why did I do that, who have I pretended to be and what was I trying to hide, etc.?

All the people I had come to know who thrived after a Perfect Storm, all of them reported having a guide, whatever form this appeared to have come in from.

The stronger their web of support in terms of the breadth and depth of relations, the more growth the individual seemed to have unlocked in a shorter period of time. Not only that, the experiences seemed to be recounted more favourably too.

The importance of this is often understated. A small insight is all it takes to trigger a whole new trajectory, but to sustain the path of growth that opened, requires enormous effort.

The more profound the learning experience, the more difficult it is to revert back to how it was before. While this could mean that the chance of sustained growth is stronger because it is more difficult to reverse, the journey is also equally strong in challenge because of that.

In any given situation, only one can understand what one experiences, only one can have one such perspective.

No two people can truly share an experience; no two people can experience similar situations in the same way, because every life is unique.

Herein lies the gift; every person, every place, every encounter, and every situation, are mirrors of our perspective.

Depending on what one chooses to work on at any point in time, every mirror can become one part of the holding structure, one part of the web of support.

A small insight is all it takes to trigger a whole new trajectory.

Therefore, space is available all the time, and the key to it lies in one's feelings.

Many of us are conditioned to react to our feelings, rather than as a portal of change. Often we want the unpleasant feelings to go away and the pleasant feelings to stay. But our feelings actually carry many messages. The capacity to use feelings as messengers can be developed.

The concept of feelings as messenger is central to how and why systemic constellations work.

There is little room for stories fabricated by personal perception when one works in a phenomenological manner; when one works with what is right here, right now.

The arrival of my daughter presented me with a fresh challenge as I found it so difficult to establish any regular formal meditation and yoga practice.

The gift of this is that I received a lot of practice in learning how to find my centre through other means.

I drew upon what I learned from breathwork and systemic constellations. I realised that to take care of myself, to hold space, meant being able to sustain my ability to notice and be in the silence between all the activities of the mind and body.

Becoming a mother surfaced a lot of emotions. On the surface, it seemed to be caused by lifestyle changes as brought on by having a baby and caring for a baby full-time.

Digging deeper, however, I learned that these emotions were all showing me what I perceived. It was showing me the gap between what I expected and what was... what my beliefs were and what I needed to believe instead.

The gaps presented new ground for my husband and I to stand on, where we need to consciously choose whether to move towards cooperation or confrontation.

- We had to learn we were both in the same team.
- We had to learn to be vulnerable with each other without blame or guilt.

There would also be no place for self-righteousness or pride.

Living with Awareness

Living with full awareness that everything is a mirror means that we can expand and extend our capacity to be and grow, by simply accessing our feelings.

It means that whenever we disregard, play down, contain, lock away, or cling to and be ruled by our feelings, we do the same to our growth... we put up obstacles or meander in our personal growth, we chase away the results of our personal growth.

By doing so, we deprive ourselves of a life that is alive, a life that is healthy, connected and satisfying, a full life that we deserve, and that is in our hands. It is in our capacity to choose conscious living. We can mobilise our Whole Capacity and expand how we live.

Reflection Points

Have you experienced a time when your world view or mental model was greatly challenged? Reflecting on it today, can you list or map out your identities, nature, choices and decisions? What does the list or map tell you about your life today?

List out your intimate relationships, past and present. What were your reasons for the break ups? What was similar in each relationship? What was different? What do you not like about your current relationship? How can this information help you today?

WAY #5: START OPENING UP TO DIFFERENT CHOICES

When we begin to live more consciously, we will start seeing choices that we never could see before.

As more choices get revealed, our life could feel like it has momentarily expanded.

We realise we can begin to be more conscious about the choices we make. In this reality, we may find that life perhaps was "simpler" when we were half-blind.

We may miss the bliss of ignorance, the time when we seemed to have less responsibility.

We may also find ourselves experiencing a lot more joy and gratitude, and by the same token, feel extra sensitive and more easily annoyed or frustrated, than before.

I spent much time investigating Choiceful Creation. It intrigues me how this element contains so much.

For instance, I was curious about the role that the amount of choices plays in enabling a life that is healthier, happier and more satisfying; is having more choice a helpful thing?

I then looked at creation and the forces enabling that. How much of what we create is due to conditioning, and how much is attributable to consciously thought through decisions? Is one way more superior than the other? Is there an alternative way?

My investigation led me to believe that Choiceful Creation is slightly different from what we could otherwise call Conscious Creation.

This is because I realise that we not only have the potential to be conscious about what we create, we can be open to infinite possibilities (even though one may argue that when we are living consciously, we become aware and therefore open to, infinite possibilities).

I felt that Choiceful Creation more accurately describes what I'm trying to convey in a sense that it operates from a place of abundance, where I believe that all of me holds the power in making a decision, and that the choices I have are determined by the choices that I can see or access at a particular point in time.

These two beliefs open the space for energy to flow where it needs to flow.

Open State

By being in an open receptive state, we may discover plenty more alternative choices that can be made:
- Choices that we may have judged in the past.
- Choices that we may not want to make but others are quite happy to.
- Choices that materialise without any laboured thought or planning on our part.

This is very different from creating out of past conditioning and without any awareness that this is so.

When we sit on the creative chair in a state of openness, we begin to ease away from control and into choices that we had seemingly chosen already, and with that, creation can begin. In coaching terms, it means getting out of our own way.

When I started working with systemic constellations, I found that the moment clients began to see the trajectory of their current situation, they begin to open up to receiving information that shows alternative choices that can be made.

I remember once, observing my own constellation and seeing the consequences of what I was doing to myself and those around me, that I did not like.

Seeing this alone helped me to see other choices I could make even if in that moment this was not consciously apparent to me. This is a kind of creative space, a high potential magical space that becomes accessible and operates as if it was a vacuum drawing out one's creativity on a blank canvas.

Think of a time when you tried to solve a problem, thinking and thinking, and just as you took a break, you had an epiphany. The creative space is rather similar.

Another example that is common is when couples ask, "Should we divorce or should we stay married and work this out?" The minute we can commit that divorce is not an option until say, three years' time, the question changes and we make way for a host of possibilities to come up that otherwise would not, had it been just the stay or split dilemma.

Creative Space

We can also experience this creative space whether sitting in silent contemplation or moving in meditation, when our mind keeps going on and we simply watch it play, or when the mind is silenced through whole body movement.

Later on, we might find an inspiration to do something different from what we would have done, had we not been in meditation, and were instead simply acting or reacting from our thoughts.

New choices show up when we allow them to.

New choices show up when we allow them to. And we allow this when we give them space to. Making a decision, given the new choices that are presented, makes the implemented choice a fuller, more encompassing one.

In doing so, we write our own story and sing our own song. We break from old patterns or past conditioning, even if the ultimate decision we make would have been the same.

This is why I spent much time investigating Choiceful Creation.

We are creating all the time, and since we are creating all the time, what would happen if we are not just conscious and open, but also curious and intuitive? What would happen if we create from a place of power?

Power as I mean it here is the belief in one's own self-worth and capacity to influence an outcome without necessarily exerting the will that comes from the ego's need to prove a point. Creating from a place of power can be so much more satisfying, with much less anxiety and stress attached to it.

Intuitive as I mean it here is the guidance that operates from the heart, from a place of possibilities, from a place of love.

This is distinct from Instinctive, which operates from the gut, from a place of survival, from a place of fear.

Intuitive means guidance that operates from the heart, from a place of possibilities, from a place of love.

Both have a rhyme and reason to exist, and both have a place in our life. Discernment of the two is the art.

Creative Energy

The key therefore is to allow our creative energy to move through and gather our whole being, our power and intuition, particularly in times of crises or personal developmental opportunity.

How do we do this?

I attended a series of intense retreats in a space of two months. They were supported either through deep intention, acoustics and pure energetic vibrations of nature, or sacred plant medicine.

During this time, I was strictly observing a raw vegan diet and fasted on several occasions. I wanted to go as deep into my subconscious as I could, to learn as much as I could, because I believed that my research for this book wouldn't be complete without this investigation.

I wanted to get to the source of loving, generative power and intuition, to befriend it in a way I never had before.

One of the retreats was held during Halloween with the leader's intention of working on darkness and shadows. I was unafraid, yet for some reason, felt intense nervous energies and it showed up as excitement and euphoria, which I felt compelled to contain.

I went in with a personal intention to integrate all of my "bodies" (I use the Kundalini Yoga framework of ten bodies for my personal development), learn how to be love, trust and joy, and to let go of expectation and fear in bringing forth the highest possible version of me... in other words, to know the source of loving, generative power and intuition in me.

I had a challenging time during the retreat. I was in such an expanded state that the experience of being eaten up and taken over by the jungle was so overwhelming that I literally choked to death and back. I was dealing with all my dark emotions all at once.

Funnily enough, I felt ecstatic the next day, until nightfall. It was as if the darkness brought back the dark experience and the emotions that surfaced for me to investigate.

I called upon my mentor and spirit guide to help me integrate and fully land. The purity of my intention was made clear to me through his words, which carried discernment and love, and it helped me map out my experience and enabled my expansion to strengthen instead of spiralling out, wasted in pain.

It became a full experience of Choiceful Creation, where it was as if my future being was unfolding right in front of me in slow motion.

Integration

The integration period was the biggest part of my learning, and I am eternally grateful to my mentor and spirit guide, and everyone who touched my process.

I focused on deeply hearing all the messages I could pick up.

All perceptions, all feelings, thoughts and judgment, were fully received, and I learned through every ounce of my being what it meant to trust myself.

Experientially, I learned what it meant to be in my own loving power.

- I learned how to be in relationship with my locus of control and intuition.
- I learned what it meant to joyfully receive, to take in, nurture and maintain, the gifts of growth.
- I learned about the dance between the guide, the seeker and the intention; the Nature of the guide, seeker and intention.

Ultimately, I learned that learning (and later on growth), could only take place because of the way choices get made.

One form of choice is similar to how we might tell ourselves to look on the bright side, or focus on the positive aspect of something, so we can speed past unpleasant feelings, which works well in everyday life.

Another form of choice feels deep and expansive. This form chooses to keep letting go of thoughts that justify or rationalise unpleasant feelings by breathing through the experience and any feelings that come up, in a way emptying the glass in preparation for what needs to fill it next.

Through this way of observation, a space for movement is allowed to open up to whatever is arising. One is then able to experience how to choicefully create reality, past, present and future.

There is a clear difference between choosing with one's intellect versus with one's whole being.

There is a clear difference between choosing with one's intellect versus with one's whole being.

Through awareness, space and movement, there is greater opportunity for threads of other possible futures to present themselves, to influence and be influenced by us.

Coming full circle, we realise that Choiceful Creation is a choice we can make.

Reflection Points

Imagine for a moment, what it would look like if you just dropped all 'shoulds' and 'wants', and focused only on pure 'needs'.... what happens?

Recall the last time you exercised a big choice. Describe it fully to yourself/someone. What were the elements in it? Did you consider the pros and cons and made a decision that was contrary to your feelings? How much did fear or euphoria play an influencing role?

WAY #6: OPENING THE PORTAL OF SEXUALITY

If you are wondering how sexuality is linked with personal, professional and organisational development, you are not alone.

So here's a choice: Take a moment to check in on how you are feeling before deciding whether to go ahead and read this chapter, or skip. That in itself is data for you.

My research into Whole Capacity and my own personal growth journey led me to a place where I had to come face-to-face with my own sexuality. It baffled me how little I knew about sexuality in general and how low my level of curiosity was for that subject.

As a society, we could definitely be more well-informed and less judgmental about sexuality as a subject and as part of where we all come from. There is tremendous shame and guilt being carried in this domain that is the source of life.

I hardly ever wondered what my beliefs around sexuality were, let alone question them, until I was in a relationship that forced me to do that.

My husband and I could discuss many topics and we had the uncanny ability to work through some very challenging differences we have encountered, until we came to our differences in sexuality.

We wanted to improve our sexual connection. Working on this brought to light the Nature of our relationship; the dance between our individual Nature. It surfaced our own individual struggles and pain points as they relate to sexuality and our sexual connection.

While this brought a greater level of intimacy and understanding, we seemed to be taking forever to improve our sexual connection. It was only years later that I came to understand that one's sexual expression is as unique as one's fingerprint, and getting to know it for one's self, let alone learning to connect with another by appreciating that fingerprint, is a lifetime's work, if this is the portal of choice for change.

As a society, we could definitely be more well-informed and less judgmental about sexuality.

In the midst of our journey to overcome our sexual challenges, my husband began to connect with the subject of sexuality very deeply, so much so that he decided to pursue a doctorate in human sexuality. In so doing, I began to get exposed to his reading materials and soon, we both became more educated about the subject, and developed a language to hold our discussions in an enlightening way.

Our sexual "problems" as we knew them to be, temporarily morphed into an adventure, and the process momentarily brought us closer.

We experienced a wide range of feelings, from excitement and joy, to worry and insecurity. We developed an appreciation of the divide and overlap between limerence, romance, lust, eroticism, intimacy, passion, sexual expression and penetrative sex.

We became even clearer about the breadth and depth of our relationship.

Sexuality as a Portal of Creation

My husband is Italian, born and raised in Castel Gandolfo in Rome. I am of Chinese heritage born and raised in the suburbs of Malaysia.

We met in London through work and when we met, we were at a similar stage of growth and the differences in our basic characteristics only made us strikingly attractive to each other.

We had over a year-long of "honeymoon" period but by the time we got engaged, our differences began to really play up in the bedroom, and we were ill-equipped to work through them.

In fact, we had known about our differences before and almost separated because of this lack of understanding of our own sexual essence. We spent over a year skirting around the issue before we began actively working at it with the help of professional third parties.

Unfortunately, the winding road was not just winding now, it was apparently forked with obstacles and apparently we had been looking in the opposite direction.

The model for psychology and therapy as it stands today is largely pathological; the client has a problem that needs to be fixed. This was how we sometimes received the help we sought.

My working-life experience however had taught me about an alternative paradigm, where the problem is a matter of perspective and restoring health does not necessarily mean digging out the root cause with the assumption that once the cause is found, health is automatically or easily restored.

Additionally, restoring health does not mean the elimination of symptoms either.

The key to restoring health begins by acknowledging what is... without judgment.

Instead, restoring health begins with the development of clarity on the gap between what is and what is desired, and why this is important for the client.

It operates at a systemic level where blocks to the client system are surfaced to be fully seen. The key to restoring health then begins by acknowledging what is... acknowledging all that is, without judgment.

Although my growing up environment did not shut down my sexuality, it did not encourage curiosity about it either.

I had developed many interests other than sexuality so that my growth was somewhat stunted in that domain.

My husband had plenty of reading to do as part of his doctorate, and so we had plenty of books coming through the post.

We were on the road when I picked up the last package that arrived for us at the hotel. I was in charge of packing, so I opened the package and found the first book that actually piqued my interest amongst the dozens he had.

It's title: "The Erotic Mind." I read the entire book on the 24-hour journey and had a breakthrough moment where I felt

I finally understood my dance, my husband's dance and our dance.

When my husband embarked on his sexology studies, I knew that our sex life would change. I was afraid that I would not be able to match up to his standards and expectations.

I mourned the death of our relationship and marriage as I had known it to be, even though I knew that we were directly working at improving it. I mourned even though I knew I did not want to return to what it was before.

This mourning was like the death of an Identity; the shrinking of an Identity into the background. It was a necessary process to open up space for a new Identity to surface.

Spinal Manipulation

During the mourning period, I got the opportunity to have my back analysed by a body-worker specialising in sexual healing.

I was fully-clothed as he poked, pushed and gently twisted my back. All of a sudden, I had my entire spine "cracked", including the one section that had never been cracked before, my sacral area.

I felt as if my whole lumbar and sacrum curvature all the way to the end of my coccyx cracked. It was a bit of a shock to the system but it did not hurt.

The whole intervention was less than 10 minutes and I felt so much better physically after that.

What I did not realise was that this gentle but deep manipulation supported my personal work by helping my body to "free up" energetic blocks.

I began to move with more fluidity and as I recognised how good that felt, I mindfully connected with the whole area whenever I remembered to.

A week later, when I read the Erotic Mind on the plane, I experienced the breakthrough moment I just described. By the time we landed, I felt as if I had moved through the Stuck State and was welcoming another Identity into my whole.

All of a sudden I felt called to experience a tantric massage in parallel with my husband, and so we made arrangements for this.

In hindsight, it seemed like we had unconsciously enacted a rites of passage.

The week that followed the tantric massage was like nothing I have ever experienced.

I felt embarrassed, as I was not familiar with going about my day filled with sexual energy.

I felt a lot of heat in my lower body that would intermittently rotate and vibrate up my back towards the neck and back down to my tailbone. Sometimes I heard wind pipes accompanied by the sensation of spinning fans behind my ears and around my scapula.

I felt hot and perpetually aroused 24 hours a day, with varying intensities. I looked at life around me and all I saw was movement, vitality and beauty. Even the patterns on the bus seat seemed to be speaking to me.

I noticed attractive men and what was attractive about them. I noticed men who were attracted to me and I did not feel shy or afraid.

My footsteps were bouncy, as if I was kissing an ever-expanding ground beneath, and that with each step a flower bloomed from under my feet.

I felt the sunlight nourishing me from my crown all the way down my legs into the ground and up.

Even though I did not feel shy or afraid, I was nervous about being 'caught' as if it was wrong to experience sexual energy in public and I felt embarrassed as I was not familiar with going about my day filled with sexual energy.

Processing

Psychologically, I was processing what had taken place… I felt the crush of all the beliefs I had identified with that were no longer true because of my life experience.

I felt confused and somewhat lost. Yet I felt energetic and vibrant, ecstatic and euphoric at the same time.

Taken together, the experience was ironic and did not make a lot of sense.

Two days later, I met a new friend at a birthday party. When we shook hands and locked eyes, an energy surged from my palms into my heart down my spine and up my ears.

Given the vibrations I was already experiencing, I didn't make much of it. Yet, somehow, we got talking and the conversation led to him mentioning an energy process that has come to be known as 'inner dance'.

Something struck me and I looked it up on the Internet. I learned that the founder, Pi Villaraza would be in town the following week, and in anticipation, I signed up for my first inner dance experience.

In the meantime, I recalled reading about the Kundalini Rising phenomenon seven years ago, so I searched for a Kundalini Yoga teacher and was to start my first series of practice too.

When I met Pi, my heart recognised something my head could not understand.

At my first session, I discovered what I wanted to find, without knowing that I was looking for it. I was moved by the intense energy that flowed through, showing me where I have "blocks", and I felt intense relief afterwards.

I decided to delve deeper, and made my way to be with the source of this work, to study the energy of this dance on a beautiful remote island in the Philippines.

Something latched to my heart as I moved effortlessly to choose and thrive on a raw vegan diet. In the week of my retreat, I was to experience my whole being as a big superconductor, "re-membering" forgotten parts of me through flowing and natural movements.

My sexual energy moved through and I began to learn about it.

- I learned to start letting go of fear and shame associated with my sexuality.
- I learned about sexual energy and how to work with it in a variety of contexts.
- I learned to stay with my sexual energy and allow it to show me what I needed to know.
- I began to learn about my feminine power that is the source of my creative power.

Live Your Whole Capacity

I kept writing, cooking, designing, and dreaming. I connected the dots in terms of my journey towards reclaiming my feminine identity.

I remembered the first intervention that unlocked this for me when I sat in a circle after my first constellation weekend with the realisation of how I had rejected the feminine in me when I held onto the systemic pain of the feminine line in my extended family system.

I felt both liberated and alive. At the same time, I was dumbfounded.

- How could I have missed this important chunk in my entire career in human development?
- How could I have completely missed out sexuality when it is a core part of every whole human being as a source of life and, by that, a source of creation?
- Could we truly and deeply develop creativity without ever looking into and including our sexuality?
- Are we correct in saying that creativity is an innate talent?

When we have the doors to creativity open, our whole being will see a whole new set of choices that previously never quite registered in our minds.

What we choose to create therefore, is fuller, more "Choice-full", than before.

I kept learning from this process and soon found a way of supporting others who wanted to embrace their identities and unlock their creative capacities in a similar way.

Rebirth

Meantime, as my husband and I emerged from this Perfect Storm, we each re-birthed our sexual identity, and we re-birthed our sexual nature and intimacy.

We experienced relief and freshness in our new-found sexual appreciation. We began to learn to choreograph our new dance. We could not rely on our old dance to inform this because the dancers and the music have fundamentally changed.

How could we develop our sexuality given our existing family structure and social schema?

Our journey has taught me that the knowledge we have gained is useful yet limited.

The labels that were helpful for learning were unhelpful when it came to choreographing our unique dance. Labels also open up a plethora of misconception and expectations from others.

We agreed that what was more important was for us to acknowledge and appreciate why, how, and what we do, to grow.

Whenever we are fully connected and loving with each other, our sexual intimacy excites and surprises us, if we are conscious enough to choose this to be. In short,

- I have learned to love my sexual energy.
- I have learned how to allow my sexual energy to show me what it wants to show me.
- I have learned to be unafraid of its powers through awareness and intuition, and put aside pride and ego.
- I discovered that when I hold a clear intention to see, my sexual energy moves towards wherever I want.

I keep discovering new things about who, how and what I want to be. I keep learning to free myself from past conditioning and respond choicefully without judgment.

I realise that without a healthy relationship with our sexuality, we cannot create well because our source power of life creation is broken.

Without a healthy relationship with our sexuality, we cannot create well.

I discovered that mastering our sexual energy is vital towards creating choicefully. This is why Sexuality is crucial in the discussion of Choiceful Creation.

The Importance of Sexuality

I placed this topic as a separate pathway from Choiceful Creation because not many people are ready to consider sexuality in this way. By doing so, I am explicitly practising Choiceful Creation.

I reconnected with the primal life forces of vitality and through a healthy relationship with sexuality, I show up from a place of loving power and deep respect to all of life.

I constantly work on sustaining this place of being, and every time I show up like this, I know I am living my Whole Capacity.

I say this because it is easy to assume that just because I have much experience with this practice, my state of happiness is permanent. My work could be easily misread as a finished product. It is not.

My husband and I thought that when we each connected to our own sexuality, and skilfully bring it to our couple, our intimacy concerns would be reframed, resolved or rendered non-existent. Well, we thought wrong.

Relief of symptoms around sexuality needs to be followed by efforts to maintain and grow oneself.

What I have come to discover is that sexuality is a form of language that leads us into an area of concern too. Just as how one might be tempted to treat anxiety, depression and compulsive obsession, these are symptoms and are languages that lead us into another person's world.

Therefore, relief of symptoms around sexuality, while positive, needs to be followed on by efforts to maintain and grow oneself, as a whole, in order for any positive change to sustain.

Life challenges are as unique as the individuals involved, therefore the language with which people come to understand their own personal problems are of course, different.

My husband is an organisational psychologist with a doctorate in human sexuality, while I have plenty of experience in deep, transformative change. One could assume we have it all figured out when it comes to human relationships. Of course not. Anyone who claims otherwise is choosing to be closed to the ever-evolving and inevitable journey of transformational growth.

As I write, my husband and I are in another perfect storm. My growth as catalysed by the last perfect storm prepared me to meet our couple life from a new place and I finally saw what

Live Your Whole Capacity

I had been blind to. I am in the "death" as I write, and this one feels massive.

What will be choicefully created from this round is anyone's guess. Perhaps this is a topic for another book. Suffice to say, the more conscious we are on this journey, and the better we are at allowing space to work its magic, the greater the likelihood that we will travel well during the perfect storm, which is crucial for the well-being of our whole system.

Whatever the outcome, one thing for certain is that, when a path to heal is choicefully created, there is no turning back to how things were. I would not want that. Growth brings about freedom and being free allows love to flow through the perceived limitations of the human form.

Blazing the trail of your own life, so to speak, calls for courage. You are the one living it, and how you choose to live it is both a duty and a birth right.

Reflection Points

When was the last time you did something self-nurturing for yourself? This could range from spending a good chunk of at least 20 minutes to cook yourself a nutritious meal, self-pleasuring or spending time in nature, to pampering spas and shopping. How connected were you to your whole being in the actions that you took?

When was the last time you had conscious sex with a partner or with yourself?

When was the last time you connected with your sexual energy and noticed the feelings or energy that come up?

On a scale of 1 to 10, with 10 being perfect and 1 being absolutely horrendous, how would you rate the quality of the connection experienced when you are experiencing the rush of sexual energy? How does this inform you today?

Ask: what am I judging about sexuality? What does this tell me about me? How might I be judging someone else's expression of their sexuality and restricting my own?

PART 3:

THE PRACTICE OF WHOLE CAPACITY

For more information and special offers, join our community at: **www.WholeCapacity.com**

BRINGING IT ALL TOGETHER

In Part 1, Whole Capacity was summarised in a nutshell.
It is about:
- Honouring and embracing all our **Identities**… every single aspect of them, whether those we attach to, those we reject or those that we are ambivalent about.
- Flowing in our **Nature** through the dance of our Identities in every context that we encounter.
- Allowing ourselves to embark on **Choiceful Creation**; the ability to choose deeply and follow through on what needs to manifest based on fresh data unfolding from living our Whole Capacity.

Process-wise, we move out of a Stuck State and go through the Perfect Storm, in birthing something new and allowing something old to move to the background.

In this part, we will discuss Immersive Living, a lifestyle made up of practices that lead to the development of one's Whole Capacity.

But before we do that, I wanted to touch upon an "open space" and the angle of "radical inclusion" with which the practice of Immersive Living would best operate.

Research and Experience

Much of what we know from mainstream psychology and psychiatry has been limited to life after birth, and the biographical experiences that occur thereafter.

Sigmund Freud and other figures of modern psychology also envisioned a personal unconscious as part of the psyche, which consists of forgotten or suppressed memories of past events and experiences.

However, research and personal experience has shown me that the psyche operates way beyond this sphere.

Two examples are perinatal experiences of birth trauma and transpersonal experiences of the archetypal, mystical or spiritual kind. These experiences cannot be removed from our psyche.

Traditional psychiatry has also been criticised and mistrusted for using a model that cannot explain many observations made in patients, such as near death experiences, spiritual crises, and out of body experiences.

Verbal psychotherapy as practised by many psychologists and psychiatrists only allows the patient to remember or reconstruct past events and experiences.

It is not uncommon for those seeking help to receive analysis and diagnosis that pointed to upbringing and genes.

Unfortunately, the belief that attributing a root cause in this way is helpful for the client's recovery, is somewhat flawed. I have encountered so many people who are stuck in this supposedly therapeutic discovery, unable to move towards healing old wounds that cut across generations, culture and tradition, purely because of the missing "open space" and "radical inclusion".

- **Open Space** is the backdrop of openness to being all of who we are, where we have come from, without shame about or desire for a different childhood experience.
- **Radical Inclusion** here means including all aspects of what we dislike about our childhood, to be honoured, respected and given a place in our human experience.

Honouring the Parents

There is great wisdom in the adage "honouring the parents".

Honouring does not mean one condones any inappropriate behaviours or disregard one's own pains and emotions.

Honouring means acknowledging what is, separating one's fate or destiny, and giving a place in one's heart for a person or situation. This is what "open space" and "radical inclusion" does.

By opening up one's heart space, there is a possibility of including all of who we are. By fully taking who they are, we finally can embrace who we are.

There was a time when like many others, I too have faulted my parents for my sorrow and disappointments in my family of origin.

Actually, this came as an improvement from a state of never allowing myself to be honest about my feelings of anger and disappointment with myself and with my parents, either by rationalizing or dismissing those "inappropriate" feelings.

When I walked the path of using myself as an instrument for change, I began to learn much more about how much power I actually have.

I began to empathise with the fallibility of my parents. I began to feel a depth of gratitude that is free from co-dependency, guilt and self-righteousness... free from merging and free from rejection.

I don't think I could have managed this level of work in such a short space of time without the support web I had. For that, I am deeply, deeply grateful.

I love my parents. That I never doubted.

What I hadn't really experienced before until the breakthrough moment was the depth of my love... the depth of a child's love for the parents, I felt when I stepped into the field of innocence that drove my actions outside the field of awareness.

Being fully present in that existential and phenomenological moment, I could experience fully all of me; all of them in me.

From that point on, I felt like I had been transported to live on a different mode. Nothing was ever quite the same.

I don't think that I would have reached this shift quite so soon if my personal work has been confined to the conversational and emotional realm of memories and rationalisation or justification, with the goal of removing pain.

What catalysed the shift in me then and continues to do so in new ways, what supports my clients today in their movement, is the energetic experience that is preverbal, that is attended to in the silence of pure awareness, free from cynicism, fear and judgement, open to infinite possibilities.

Why Is This Kind Of Personal/Self Work So Important?

It is important because it is "coming home".

The groundedness and sense of security we embalm in, and our ability to set foot somewhere and grow healthy roots, lies in the capacity we gain as a result of fully taking in our source of life.

If we desire to live with deep contentment, experience joy and profound love, the only way is to meet our source of life.

Our vitality, our freedom from the prison of our stories, our compassion for the suffering of humanity, and our essence as lived in this human experience, are greatly if not wholly dependent upon how we relate, multi-dimensionally, with our parents.

If we desire to live with deep contentment, experience joy and profound love, the only way is to meet our source of life.

All our perceived pains and blocks are signposts that guide us there like a map. Our uniqueness means that we each have our own unique path.

From my experience, this source of life has been described to me in the following ways:

- My Perinatal Experience
- My Sexuality
- Self-Love
- My Parents
- God
- The Pure Light Within
- The God in Me
- My Imprint
- My Inner Compass
- My Calling
- My Breath

- My Soul
- My Family
- My Spirit
- Mother Earth
- My Essence etc.

Whenever we reject our source of life, and we all do that, in that moment we cannot live our Whole Capacity.

The more we meet and integrate our source of life, the more we embody our fullness, the more we live our Whole Capacity, the more content, love and joy we experience.

The infusion of this with the choices we choose to create elevates the game we play, where we can call bluff the separateness we constructed out of fear.

On a practical note, we choose what promotes life, not what kills it.

IMMERSIVE LIVING: THE PRACTICE OF LIVING YOUR WHOLE CAPACITY

It pains me to know that many of us are not encouraged to immerse ourselves fully in life, to live fully engaged and connected with all of life.

Being able to do that is the practice of living your Whole Capacity, what I call Immersive Living

There's plenty of evidence that suggest we are programmed to seek to live. Ironically, in doing so, we unconsciously programme avoidance of death, even if our actions may suggest otherwise or we claim to be unafraid of dying.

When faced with choice, we may find that we feel one thing, think another and decide something else.

> *When we say "Yes" to something, we are also saying "No" to something else.*

If we can make this conscious, we can give Immersive Living a chance.

Many of my client-colleagues are unaware of their lives having been shaped to avoid "making mistakes" or "failing", and consequently, they live with underlying anxiety and guilt over bringing shame.

It is not uncommon to find these individuals holding onto the burden that is causing them pain almost as a barometer of who they are.

Interestingly, I have found that those who reject the burden placed on them are also not free from the pain. The price of this is the depletion of energy, if not confidence and personal conviction, and the promotion of self-doubt and feelings of being trapped.

These client-colleagues are not equipped to penetrate through personal challenges and expand their way of living.

In an earlier chapter, I mentioned Use of Self as an instrument of change.

The same analogy can be used as a way to frame an experience. Whenever we bring our locus of control back into ourselves, if it had begun to spiral out towards blame or attachment, we open up a possibility of seeing any experience, particularly painful ones, as a way of refining our instrumentality.

It is not uncommon to find individuals holding onto the burden that is causing them pain almost as a barometer of who they are.

Taken this way, we lead ourselves to drive our vehicle of growth in this journey called life. We change how we live from a potentially passive and victimised way, to an expansive life-giving one, filled with vitality.

This is why Immersive Living underpins all the elements. Yet because it is the backdrop, the canvas, the field behind that can remove those blinkers or veil and support all the other building blocks, it is easy to miss.

The 12 Senses

Immersive Living, at its foundation, calls for all our traditional senses of sound, sight, touch, smell, and taste, to be open and engaged, and for us to work with a mind that is balanced in its development.

Without this base, it is more challenging to develop other subtler senses. An over-developed thinking mind, for example, often comes at the expense of full development of the other senses.

To expand the way we live, we can start by working with a bigger picture of our senses.

There are many theories but I like to use the 12 senses approach first described by Rudolf Steiner over 90 years ago. It parallels with Howard Gardner's Multiple Intelligences education theory.

The 12 senses are:
- **Sense of Touch**: Inner sense of "where I end and the outer world begins," an internal response to a contact from the outside world.
- **Sense of Life**: Inner sense of one's own feeling of well-being, of being alive, a way of sensing the nutritional difference between fresh raw vegetables and over-boiled vegetables.
- **Sense of Movement**: Inner sense of the way body parts move in relationship to each other.

- **Sense of Balance**: Inner sense of one's own equilibrium and stability, to orientate with respect to directions like up, down, right, and left.
- **Sense of Smell**: Middle sense allowing one to come in contact with the outside world through odours.
- **Sense of Taste**: Middle sense allowing deeper connection with the outside world through flavours.
- **Sense of Sight**: Middle sense that takes in images of the outside world.
- **Sense of Warmth**: Middle sense allowing direct awareness of the warmth of another body.
- **Sense of Hearing**: Higher sense allowing us to receive the resonance of an object, through which we learn about the inner structure of something we see.
- **Sense of Language**: Higher sense of speech or word or tone, hearing that involves meaningful words.
- **Sense of Thought**: Higher sense of entering the being speaking through their words.
- **Sense of Ego**: Higher sense of ego enabling us to turn towards the being of another and hold their ego, their unique individuality.

Using these 12 senses to map our daily experience of life, we open the doors to engage our whole being on a regular basis, and thus, the capacity to receive the gifts of Immersive Living.

- Without a healthy sense of touch, life and movement, for example, one cannot really feel fully alive, in the body and in connection with other beings.
- Without a healthy sense of hearing, language and ego, one cannot really fully empathise and connect with all of life.

Live Your Whole Capacity

Fully Immersed

Immersive Living breathes life to the elements of Whole Capacity.

Being fully immersed in life helps us appreciate the full powers of knowing and working with Identity, Nature and Choiceful Creation.

To live is to show up in life with your whole being.

This is also why Immersive Living evidences Whole Capacity.

To live is to show up in life with your whole being.

Therefore, it doesn't matter whether one chooses to view practices for personal growth like meditating, setting intention, making commitment and taking action, attending development workshops or retreats, as tools, or as part of one's daily living.

As long as one shows up fully in life, with all senses open, one opens up the doors to living one's Whole Capacity.

Sitting on the fence with a decision, while this could be a Choiceful Creation in and of itself, is not Immersive Living.

On the other hand, making a decision in accordance with the choices available, without pressure, while knowing that one does not have all the information that one needs to feel totally comfortable, is Immersive Living. Both are different states and therefore changeable.

Choosing to stay in an "unhealthy" relationship out of fear of what it would be like otherwise, is not Immersive Living. But choosing to remain in an "unhealthy" relationship with the commitment and/or conviction of both parties to free themselves of entanglements, is Immersive Living.

Choosing to not do a particular course for practical reasons, yet not deepening an understanding of the drivers, is not very aligned with Immersive Living. But choosing to set an intention to be open to life's opportunities to learn could turn it into Immersive Living.

Practising Immersive Living

The big question is: how can we get in the habit of practising Immersive Living?

How can we develop the awareness, courage and effort to act beyond the zone of comfort?

How can we keep doing this, better and better?

I wish to offer an idea that we can do this by improving our core capacity to SEE, i.e. to Sense, Engage and Experiment.

- **Sense**

    Our capacity to sense influences our experience of life. The richness of life is available to us when we can tune into its frequencies.

    The 12 senses can help frame the development of this capacity. We grow new sense organs that have more than just one physical body part attached to it.

    For example, our capacity to sense movement doesn't simply involve our brain. We develop an invisible "organ" to sense movement that consists of the brain and more. It includes the meta-physical.

- **Engage**

Our capacity to engage, to connect deeply with life, is influenced by how open we are in terms of our whole being... How open-minded we are, how open-hearted we are, and how willing we are.

For example, to establish a newer more healthful behaviour, we need to be open-minded to try something that is perhaps unacceptable in our culture at one point in time.

We need to be able to do this wholeheartedly and be open to all emotions that arise. And we need to take that first step and mobilise our whole being into action.

- **Experiment**

    Our capacity to experiment refers to the expansion of our will to act. It involves adopting a learning stance to life, to accept that we are always a 'work in progress', to receive feedback as feedback, and to renew our determination to remain playful and curious about life and how we choose to live our lives.

    It means mustering the courage as necessary to face any fears, to let go of expectations and the need to have control over an outcome. It is the art of taking action.

    For example, if I wanted to improve my relationship, I would want to consider my current situation as something I am experiencing today, that it is part of a process rather than an end-state.

- I would want to receive all feedback instead of deflecting it with my defensive shield.
- I would want to take any action I deem necessary even if I feel frightened.
- I would want to let whatever that wants to come from my action to be what it wants to be.

A Dozen Tips to Developing Whole Capacity

There is plenty that can be done to support the development of our Whole Capacity. I'm sharing 12 tips here as a starting point.

1. **Consider the whole and play our part in shaping a space that supports the people in it to live the best that they can live.**

    As one enters the practice of Immersive Living, one learns to live more expansively and to life-dance every single day. In doing so, the experience of life changes as one begins to see parts of a system as an ecology that shapes and is shaped by its own environment.

    When we enter a meeting, we begin to see the heritage represented in the room, the invisible forces that push or pull in one direction or another, the love that is seeking to be restored in a more healthful way, the place one is placed compared to where one could be placed to enable flow, etc.

    Given this, one can then choose where and how to intervene or let be.

Decide to drop the blinkers or veil and soon enough, with the right support, one can have this practice become second nature.

2. **Explore our personal or individual system.**

   The journey to discovery of one's identities is an adventure too precious to pass. As one embarks on this, one learns to differentiate facts versus opinions.

   There are so many ways to explore this... I have catalysed and guided many journeys using a wide range of processes, from vanilla talent management work in organisations, to highly personalised interventions such as a combination of breath, movement, and body work, group dialogue, and systemic coaching.

   Various forms of transition support come in handy in times of big change, such as when we become the new mother, father, manager, entrepreneur, trailing spouse, sexually frustrated, or disillusioned and/or generally disconnected from who we are.

   But we do not need to wait for a 'crisis' before deciding to discover our identities and welcome our highest possible version. In fact, we can choose to choicefully create whenever we feel called to.

3. **Increase awareness of self and others.**

   Nothing is more important in the establishment and maintenance of healthy boundaries and energy than awareness.

   Being mindful helps move us out of cruising through life on auto-pilot. Meditating helps us discern between all our inner and outer dialogue participants. Being reflective and journaling can help us make sense of self and others.

Learning to lean back and listen instead of lean in and listen, the way we are taught to show or do active listening, can help us take in more non-verbal information.

Examining our systemic constellations from time to time can help raise awareness of hidden dynamics playing up at home and at work.

4. **Revitalise our mind.**

    Engage in activities that stock our minds with delicious memories so they sustain us throughout life. Dance, move the body, listen to or make music, celebrate seemingly small life events, do anything that helps bring one into conscious awareness.

    Concentrate on finding solutions instead of seeking problems. Decide what mood we want to be in and choose to create conditions for this mood to arise and grow.

    Choose to experience vitality in everything and everyone we come in contact with. Develop appreciation for the ordinary so the extraordinary can come about.

5. **Aim for 80:20 with our choice of fuel, keeping knowledge up to date about nutrition and practice moderation.**

Make an assessment of where we are with regards to our diet and pick an 80:20 to experiment with.

For example, based on your current conditions, perhaps you can experiment with going 80% organic, or 80% meat-free, or 80% raw, or 80% vegetarian, or 80% vegan, as a way of learning about the dance between the many versions of ourselves with food or culture or expectations.

Other examples include choosing to go 80% alcohol-free, 80% cigarette-free, 80% dairy-free, or 80% internet-free for a period of time, as an experiment and a learning journey.

My journey from being caloric-focused to nutrition-focused, from meat to fish to seafood to vegetarian to whole foods to vegan, to how foods are cooked, body-mind detox and spiritual fasting, and from going on and off self-designed programmes, has given me rich insight into my whole well-being, to influence all my choices beyond foods.

I believe that food is an accessible tool available to many of us for transformative change. Our body contains 23,000 human genes, in contrast to over one million bacterial genes. Microbiome, mostly in our gut, holds the key to changing our future.

6. **Wherever possible, choose a personal coach, therapist, mentor, manager or guide who can take in your wholeness, who can see your whole person.**

There is plenty of evidence in support of the view that you are more than a physical bag of bones with an ego.

Even if you choose to believe you are simply a physical bag of bones with an ego, it does no harm to find a resource (someone who supports you in life that is outside your immediate circle of family and friends) who can see or experience you as a collection of systems or bodies.

This person will add much richness to your experience of life by tuning in to co-existing parts and, in doing so, broadcast this back to you such that, over time, you can learn to receive it. In any case, you will learn something even if you do not grow from it.

Learning can be a given but growth only comes with choice.

7. **Practice MOCK parenting filled with Love. Imagine interactions with oneself as a child.**

    How might one be as a MOCK parent - Mindful, Open, Curious and Kind? Imagine interactions with others where one can also see the children in the others.

    How might one be a MOCK parent to the children in others? Are we able to "parent" with love? Are we able to distinguish between acts of love that support their growth through total acknowledgement and acceptance, versus acts of love that soothe parental guilt, that give in to the demands of, and therefore spoil, the children?

Live Your Whole Capacity

How about acts of love that make us feel good and helpful versus acts of love that actually enable others to feel good and strong about themselves? Are we able to shower massive love that will not spoil the children?

8. **Be our own guardian and guardian of our partner's secure base**

   As we learn about our own basic childhood fears, and that of our partners, we can learn about our trigger points and therefore communicate in a way that the one owning the trigger points can feel safe.

   Stan Tatkin's book "Wired for Love" is an excellent resource to learn how to do this.

   By inviting the guardian identities into our most intimate relationship, we foster a deep sense of safety in our nature, a sense of safety that many of us long for, which support us in bringing out the best in each other, and allows us to truly spread our wings and soar.

9. **Establish our own space as an individual and as a family.**

   Learning to carve out personal space in the midst of the technologically-enhanced busyness and over-connectedness, is an art.

   Take time to engage in activities that one enjoys, on one's own, separate from the partner or families. Spend time either with non-mutual friends or with mutual friends separately.

This is important in terms of maintaining healthy differences and boundaries.

Without this, blinkers and veils start to develop causing us to see less.

Interest in and attraction to each other also wanes, and when these wane, not only does intimate connection suffer but we cannot grow our Whole Capacity.

Some people develop surrogate families but being able to establish your own space means negotiating membership into these families on one's own terms too.

10. **Choose experiences versus increasing possessions.**

    There's research that suggests choosing to buy experiences instead of things actually increases the rate of happiness in people.

    My husband and I decided in our first year together that we will prioritise experiences in our gifts selection process, and since then, we have built a reservoir of shared experiences that continue to nourish and sustain us till today.

    I am almost certain that had we not done more than half of them, we wouldn't be where we are today.

    The more experiences we have, the more likely we are to create conditions for us to grow our Whole Capacity.

11. **Experience others as mirrors. What we see is driven by our perception.**

We create our own reality (what I mean by reality is how we experience life). We therefore own our own reality, and we can use what we experience as our reality to inform us in our own growth.

When we learn to see others as mirrors, when we begin to experience our interaction with them as mirrors of us, we start to develop a more sophisticated internal locus of control. We accept all that we are seeing and experiencing, whether we like them or not, as a reflection of us... parts of us that we embrace, and parts of us that we reject.

It allows us to collect them all and integrate into us across all dimensions of time and space. It allows us to practice self-love, which in turn helps us expand our Whole Capacity.

12. **Learn to develop and work with symbols and rituals.**

    Some of our deepest longings, the cravings that came about in the course of one's biographical life or evolution of the human race, could turn into major gaps in life as we grow older, screaming to be acknowledged and filled.

    In my personal growth journey, there were numerous occasions where I came face-to-face with the magnetic pull into the void, occasions where I couldn't seem to move on.

    As I began to understand some of these deep longings, I could see how I was latching onto the wrong fillers as I battled the strong pull towards fulfilment of these deep longings.

Through my experience, I learnt to apply the powers of symbols and rituals as practiced by native tribes, in my personal, individual and organisation development work.

For example, my client-colleague and I designed a ritual that once completed, would symbolically mark her rites of passage in becoming a woman as well as an adult daughter in relation to her parents. She looked, felt and sounded remarkably different as she stepped into the current, new stage of life, in retrospect. The feedback we got was astounding.

There's the whole dozen! If you develop your own, do share with me, I would love to hear them!

PART 4:

APPLICATION

For more information and special offers, join our community at: **www.WholeCapacity.com**

APPLICATIONS OF WHOLE CAPACITY

The practice of Whole Capacity applies across personal and professional domains, whether in innovation and leadership development, or in relationships, marriage and parenting.

Creating and enabling an environment that supports the development of one's Whole Capacity can be the result of clear unwavering intention that is held dear.

In this segment, we look in more detail at applications in the following:
- Business and Organisations
- Intimate Relationships
- Parenthood and Childhood

APPLICATION #1: WHOLE CAPACITY IN BUSINESS AND ORGANISATIONS

When I decided to work with people instead of numbers, I was galvanised by the potential for positive change I could have on people's lives.

I could help businesses and organisations find the right people, help keep them learning, growing and loving their employers, and if things didn't work out, support people with redeployment and outplacement. I was totally confident in my ability to deliver on that.

As time went by, I realised increasingly that the skills required of me were not exactly that.

It had more to do with my ability to read people, analyse the ecology of the business and organisations, determining my place and permission in the system, finding courage and developing a tolerance for not being liked... than my technical ability to do my job.

The reality that the organisation is made up of highly personal systems of individuals interacting with varying degrees of influence, hierarchies and protocols, with each other, and as a result, creating an organisation system with a life force of its own... further complicates matters yet also simplifies in a sense that once acknowledged, there is great vitality that can be released.

When this creative life force of the organisation comes out to play, the possibilities of what the collective, the organisation, can achieve, is infinite.

Many of the perceived problems can be creatively resolved when flow is restored in the organisation as effected when a systemic approach is taken.

The challenge often is that this calls for a higher understanding by custodians of the organisation. It is not uncommon therefore to find finger-pointing and learned helplessness in the light of problems.

When fear is the dominant energy running in the system, creative life force is compromised, and the only thing that pulses is slow decay.

Perception and Honesty

Being privy to conversations across all levels of the organisation, I was astounded by the big difference in perception and honesty.

The higher up the hierarchy, the more the quality of perception and honesty diminish. Fear is greater and smaller at the same time, for while the stakes are higher, the individual power in the organisation is also greater than the mass population.

Still, the information that flows down and up the chain of command is so filtered; no wonder that the price paid for this is trust.

As long as business performance (chiefly financial) targets are being met, nothing else really matters.

Live Your Whole Capacity

Not many would boldly question, for example, whether the people we are losing have a certain characteristic that we wanted to bring to the organisation in the first place and what makes us do this.

When targets are not being met, people are punished or booted out. Not many would boldly question the many alternative possibilities of this. It seems as if organisations operate with the assumption that there is always someone to assign blame... someone to take the blame.

The dish of the day in organisations is a mentality of scarcity, rather than abundance; the mentality of survival, competition and/or profit-making, at all cost, with regards to all things external to the organisation.

There is a clear disconnect with any sense of "higher" purpose or the nature of this "angel" or "beast" in society and communities world-over... at a cost. It is less challenging today to experience the price paid for yesterday's ignorance because of the changes storming through large systems like banking, pharmaceutical and agricultural systems.

But if we operate with Whole Capacity in mind, we can capture the essence that the collection of personal systems, co-existing and interacting with each other, have identities that are either accepted as belonging there or are rejected or excluded and therefore seeking redress.

We can appreciate the nature of our business; that our business or organisation has a way of relating with the external world. We can wonder what our business or organisation is actually creating and whether this is done choicefully or blindly.

The Road Less Travelled

Change starts from within, through teams and groups and dedicated projects, whether on-going day-to-day, or ad hoc, through large scale initiatives.

Taking the road less travelled may get lonely and exhausting, and I am humbled by those I met who would boldly show up for what they believed and stood for.

In my work with organisations, I have witnessed the power that great managers have in turning around the work experience and productivity of their staff. Some of these great managers often identify strongly with the role of caretaker or guardian, or inspiring leader.

When Oberdan joined the UK retail arm of a large international bank, he became responsible for the learning and development of 40,000 people in 1400 branches, and inherited a team of seven, most had been in the organisation for at least 11 years with one hitting 38 years of tenure.

The move to this role meant that for the first time, he transitioned from being an individual contributor to having a team to lead, in a context that was rather different from his previous role.

While he revelled at the possibilities of what can be achieved by virtue of having a team, and the performance management aspects of the role came naturally to him, the portfolio size as well as the situation he inherited challenged him. He says:

> *"There was no structure, no plans, the team was working on a reactive basis and only up to three months of a journey ahead without having a clear picture of the stakeholders nor accountability.*

My team consisted of people who had a set way of working and all of whom had been beaten up to be quiet and do as they are told.

My team expected me to take them step-by-step, so this was a shock on both parties. There was also no leadership above me to tell me about priorities and my manager was focused on a project that had nothing to do with the rest of her team.

It ultimately took a full year to get some sort of structure in place. I prioritised restructuring the team, clarifying roles and portfolios, spent time with each to communicate, educate and coach what their roles meant and how I needed them to work from that point onwards.

In addition to monthly one-to-one coaching, I had a quarterly team event and brought experts to help my team work from a place of strength. These were people embedded in the status quo, I brought a breath of fresh air but it was a difficult shift to make. The role was tough but it gave me great satisfaction. My job evolved to one with minimal operational involvement and maximum coaching effort.

It was enormously rewarding to see the team move from being scared little children to adults making decisions and owning their portfolio.

The team became extremely gelled, working with a clear heartbeat in the direction set. The team engagement score went from 50% to 80% independent of any intervention of my part.

We set up cleaner processes and established the

first learning council owned by the business who would supervise all requests. We won multiple industry awards for the programmes we created that established a direct link between our learning interventions to revenue growth.

Personally, it raised my understanding of my capabilities as a leader and manager of others and how much more effective I am in this space compared to when I was an individual contributor.

It consolidated my belief that many Corporates don't know how to promote, don't know how to distinguish between leadership and management, don't know how to operate beyond managing day-to-day operations. Intellectually, the role was not particularly challenging, but emotionally it was hugely challenging.

I felt abandoned and unimportant in the eyes of the leaders, and it appeared as if teams were being set up to fight other teams to see who can survive the madness. I became fiercely protective of my team and my space.

That experience helped me grow enormously. As a person who finds it impossible to ask for help, I still managed to get a lot of help, which is one of the reasons I was successful and I grew. I got help from the consultant who became a coach, confidante.

I grew as a manager, as a leader, and as a man. I grew in confidence and I eventually learnt that this is because I was more suited to leading others than operating as an individual contributor.

The more I did in that role and, after that, the more I got to test myself in the world, the more I became an adult. I occupied more of my space, and my identity became clearer to myself and those around me.
Several years on, I can say it is like this, but when I was in it, all I could experience was pain. On reflection, I realise that's what growth is."

Oberdan stepped into a new identity and discovered his nature in the perfect storm he was in, such that he chose to create a different reality for himself and his team.

The Whole Capacity of his team grew from his high-touch approach to leading his team.

Exercise

1. Draw or imagine your project or team set up.
2. Who is present today, in the here and now?
3. Do you have a safe container? Is anyone being exposed?
4. Can you all "breathe" well? Is anyone feeling threatened, burdened or suffocated?
5. How do you "dance" with each other? Does it flow?
6. How do you "dance" with others external to your set up?
7. What comes up for you? Any reflections? What are you committing to? What have you learned here and how can you apply it?

APPLICATION #2: WHOLE CAPACITY IN INTIMATE RELATIONSHIPS

Intimate relationships offer the possibility of healing at a very deep level.

What I mean by healing is the relief or dissolution of internally held tension. It is different from the pathological viewpoint that we have broken parts that need to be fixed.

Intimate partners are the closest mirrors that help us see our greatest possibilities.

As more constructs are introduced over the course of the partnership, for example, engagement, spiritual or religious ceremonies, marriage or civil partnership, parenthood, sponsorship, separation, divorce, sexual openness, polyamory, or death, more identities get birthed, brought to the foreground or pushed to the background, each continuously dancing with the other's.

The nurturing of the individuals' separate growth, and that of the partnership together, is important in helping the union to choicefully create and allow what wants to emerge to come forth.

When two people come together in a relationship, they each bring with them all of their past and present relationships (previous partners, family of origin and ancestry).

From a systemic point of view, they each come into their relationship in presence of their system. This is an inescapable fact.

All the feelings that come to surface only reveal the dynamics of each of their systems, as well as the new system that is emerging from their dance.

When one grows, the other can either see or not see this changing person. If this growth is seen, the other could be inspired and learn to meet this 'new' person. If this growth is not seen, the couple could start separating from each other. And vice versa.

Daily Interactions

In a couple's daily interactions, there often is the temptation to believe that our feelings are caused by what our partner has done.

While our feelings are indeed triggered by specific instances, a similar situation might not trigger the same feelings in another person. Therefore, it cannot be that our partners are the cause.

Feelings that are triggered by something external can be described as secondary feelings. The primary feelings only show up when we peel into another layer to consider what is it that we believe about ourselves in relation to the situation.

I am not suggesting that there are never any inappropriate behaviours as such, but the causes leading up to either primary or secondary feelings are usually larger than what our partner did or did not do.

Our initial attraction to our romantic partners is likely to have in it, amidst the falling-in-love hormones, a belief that one of our core needs will be met by this person.

It is very common to find similarities in the couple to their parents coupling, even if on the surface the union looks different, therefore increasing the chances of unhealthy patterns being repeated across generations.

Paradoxically, it would seem that intimate relationships provide an abundance of opportunities to stop unhealthy patterns from repeating. Not only would this serve the future generation, history could even be "rewritten" to some extent.

This is why I am passionate about systemic work as it applies to intimate relationships.

The dance between people in intimate relationships offers such richness of experience and opportunities for growth to the individuals involved. Intimate relationships can be the bedrock to evolutionary growth of humanity.

At the beginning of many romantic relationships, there is often a degree of limerence, a state experienced when one is intensely attracted to another and have thoughts, fantasies or desires for reciprocity and to have a relationship with the person.

The language that is commonly used to describe this is 'to fall in love'. 'Love' is a misnomer, even if 'fall' is accurate insofar as describing the helplessness or obsession that is experienced.

If a full-on healthy romantic relationship develops from this, the couple feels sexy, ecstatic and strong. Over time, love, intimacy and trust can grow.

As love, intimacy and trust grow, the way the couple relates with each other and the world begins to take a form of its own, giving rise to the third entity called the relationship.

As each partner feeds the relationship, they give up a bit of themselves in the process. In order for them to remain attracted to each other, they each need to continue to grow in their own person, separate from their coupling and outside of their relationship.

Growing as a Couple

Both my husband and I have grown tremendously as individuals and as a couple since we met. In our time together, we have welcomed many identities and evolved our way of relating with each other.

We both believe that we have grown stronger individually and as a couple over the years. The reason for this is that we managed to keep the rate with which we grew as an individual and as a couple at about the same pace, through effort and patience.

We keep learning to develop our capacity to be together as whole persons.

My husband and I met at a time when we were at roughly a similar stage of growth. We were aware of what we were working on within ourselves and found in each other what we needed to feel accepted and supported to continue with our personal work, which was comforting and validating.

With both of us being in the human development field, we were also very interested in what each other had to say and very inclined to help each other grow.

Our stark personality, background and cultural differences did not seem to matter as we celebrated our passion and homecoming. It was as if we found a new home; different from our family of origin yet familiar enough.

We both have a need for stability and adventure. We value freedom and togetherness, and honour our own truths.

Two years later, my husband proposed at the end of a four-day hike up Machu Picchu. It was something I wanted and waited for, yet when it happened, I was caught surprised and silenced into surrealism.

All of a sudden, I felt nervous. My focus on "securing safety", which was tied to a marriage commitment, overshadowed any other thoughts that had already been on my mind about what it meant to me to marry him. I couldn't fully relax into and enjoy my engagement period.

I entered a transition within a transition and moved towards coming to terms with all the fears residing with me, some mine, many not. Ultimately, I was dealing with a primal fear of being abandoned.

Clarity

By working with a few people I trust, I developed clarity about my predicament. I stepped into my second marriage with enough lightness of heart, confidence and freedom. I changed my last name and embraced our new adventure together.

I welcomed the opportunity to discover the world through another lens… and that came with laughter, tears and everything in between… as a wife.

I hadn't really investigated what kind of wife I saw myself becoming. Ten months into our marriage, my husband got a job in Singapore. I became a trailing partner, fully dependent on the spouse, pregnant and not working.

In retrospect, I found myself doing things that seemed to jive with what I believed was the role of a wife, even as I busied myself with my own project and prepared for our baby's arrival.

With the systemic pull, I felt increasingly unattractive to my husband and less worthy as I engaged in activities that did not contribute economically to our family of soon-to-be three.

As the weight of home admin shifted more and more towards my side while my husband earned the dough, we were both lured into the dynamic we were familiar with in our family of origin.

We began to feel distant and disconnected from each other, and we started to trigger each other in a way we hadn't before. We realised that a new depth of personal work was called for.

We received help from a fellow colleague to understand the dimensions of our intimacy, the challenges our transition had brought to us, and to do our own self-work separately.

We kept evolving a system of being together and allowing conflict to do its job. Impatient to see improvements, we had to learn to focus on the process and help each other recognise and acknowledge our slow steady shifts.

Over time, our knowledge and understanding of each other's "systems" grew in breadth and depth.

We kept having to practice generosity at heart and prudent investment in our relationship by sharing our inner selves and what we learnt from the outside.

We struggled but still sat with each other through the most trying times in our relationship even when this was against our preference at that time.

We had to keep learning to appreciate each other's main struggles and we almost always, eventually, reached empathy with a renewed resolve to "do it better next time".

Celebration

Over time, we became better at celebrating each other's individuality and encouraged activities that would take away couple time especially if it supports personal growth.

We learnt to focus on the larger pie that is working for us whenever a slice of it became problematic. We kept the dialogue, no matter how frustrating it was.

Through one dialogue, we discovered that even though we may sometimes feel that our relationship is not where we each wanted it to be, it is beautiful precisely for that reason; we figured that our relationship is the third entity in our couple system containing parts of each of us, and that it cannot and will not contain all of us in it.

One valuable mirror of our relationship is our daughter, and she mirrors the health of our relationship.

One fine day, we came across an old photograph of us. We both said, "Wow", and looked at each other, pleasantly surprised and slightly proud of how much we have grown.

We looked more "adult", not in the physical sense (save for the additional wrinkles!) but in how much more comfortable we are in our own skin, how much more attractive we are, and how deeply connected and devoted we are to each other today.

It was a beautiful moment, etched in my mind forever.

The key to developing the capacity to be together as whole persons is three-fold:

- On-going practice of seeing and taking each other as each are, at any point in time.
- Learning about and respecting one's own and each other's boundaries.
- Trusting that the individual growth serves the couple.

It is noticeable how couples who can do this tend to get better at being together. Logically, it makes sense. Emotionally, it may even feel counter-intuitive.

Our biology seeks patterns as a way of understanding and finding comfort. Therefore, we may not easily see the subtle changes in a person, let alone an intimate partner whom we spend naked time with, psychologically and physically.

We may not have learnt how to shift our boundaries in a healthy way, let alone learn our partner's while moving ours. We also may not see that spending more time apart could directly serve us.

In an intimate relationship, who and what we are, i.e. all of our evolving identities and nature, are lived with the least of facades.

Honesty is worth honouring and when fully taken into our hearts with deep gratitude, the way in which we live will flow and keep changing for the better.

We will feel larger and live larger, not in an egoistic way, but ordinarily strong and loving in a powerful yet humbling way. We experience the other like no other and it is a privilege that brings an all-serving purpose.

Today, I work with couples who are committed to growth… couples who want to break through their differences in background, culture, energy, and life philosophy, shape their shared life, and profoundly grow.

The fact that couples are still together, storm after storm, is not how I measure of success even if this is perhaps what becomes inspiring to others.

It is more the quality of life as a couple and as a family that acts as a barometer of success. This implies a concept that success is a state of health in togetherness.

Should a marriage ever end in divorce, in my mind, this is no indicator that the marriage failed. In a similar vein, remaining married is no indicator that the marriage is a success.

Marriage at its worst is a contract governed by law and subject to games being played. Marriage at its best is a spiritual union or partnership in life governed by openness and trust. In both scenarios, love exists in various forms.

Reaching a forked path and choosing a different one halfway through the marriage course is a reality everyone lives with regardless of the intention.

Reflection Points

1. What about your partner are you happy with?
2. What about you are you unhappy with?
3. What are you unfulfilled with in your relationship?
4. What irritates you most when you argue?
5. How do you cope with stress, fear or pain?
6. When you look at your partner, who else comes to mind?
7. What do all these say about me?
8. At suitable opportunities, try leaning back to take in the other person when listening, instead of leaning in to actively pick up details of what the other person is saying. Feel for the difference.

APPLICATION #3: WHOLE CAPACITY IN PARENTHOOD AND CHILDHOOD

Many children today are robbed off their childhood by well-meaning adults who believe they are giving their children a head start.

In some countries, children are expected to know how to read and write by the time they start primary school around the age of six.

The belief that balance is achieved by developing the physical, emotional and intellectual capacities of a young child all at the same time, through chunks of activities targeting each capacity separately, is pervasive in the collective system.

In general, it is very difficult to transcend the education system in order to make it work for every unique student within it.

Long before I became pregnant, I developed a keen interest in perinatal experience, Bowlby's attachment theory, and the educational philosophy of Rudolf Steiner, out of my work as a leadership assessor and coach.

Given that our growth imprint from pre-birth shapes our continuous development into adulthood, I was deepening my understanding of human development to sharpen my instrumentality for the work I was doing. I reflected on my own perinatal experience, attachment base and education, and how I have been developing as a leader and human being, from that melting pot.

When I later became pregnant, the way I carried my pregnancy was heavily influenced by my learning in this area.

As my husband and I continued to grow, the way we chose to birth our daughter reflected our belief that babies carry birth imprints into their adult lives, and the way we chose to raise our daughter only kept evolving with the addition of direct experience.

While stepping into parenthood consciously with our whole being meant that we each entered the perfect storm at the same time, it did not mean an argument-free, totally understanding and romantic time with baby because our relationship also entered the perfect storm.

As we processed deeply personal changes, we turned into the easiest counterpart for each other's blames and triggers.

New Identity

When we become parents, a new identity enters each of our lives individually and together. This expansion means that we need to have space to accommodate it, and space is opened up by virtue of raising the game of our internal locus of control.

If we do not develop our internal locus of control, we can easily lose our energy for growth and choose to run away from unpleasant experiences rather than transcend them.

Such an action may not necessarily help us get to the root of the problem and resolve deeper, more complex, issues impacting our interpersonal and intrapersonal relationships.

Live Your Whole Capacity

Becoming a parent brings to the foreground the child identity as the closest parallel, in an effort to make sense of the change. At its best, it brings to the foreground, curiosity around parenthood and healing of old wounds.

This commonly involves walking the new terrain with your partner, while your inner worlds are being rehashed. The course is similar, but not the same, and without suitable support structure, the journey is much rougher.

When my first child was born, my husband and I and our new journey together were also born as father, mother, and parents. I held views about how I wanted to be a mother, and likewise he held views about how he wanted to be a father.

We never sat down to discuss how we wanted to be parents together. We must have assumed our ways of parenting would naturally and easily fall into place since we both got along and knew that we each wanted to be the best father and mother we could be. But it didn't.

I experienced some of the most hormonally-charged and exhaustion-multiplied post-natal "craziness" I ever had in my entire life, in the early weeks and months. I was feeling joyful one minute, sad, angry or impatient at another.

My husband was also at his most vulnerable, sensitive and defensive. Sophisticated as we were in how we communicated and handled conflicts in the past, this combination when played over new terrain, led to storms that seemed to be the last straw whenever they thundered.

It took corralling support and consistently choosing patience, perseverance and commitment, plus a paradigm shift, to open up the space that could accommodate our expansion, for our intended future together to be created in.

New Parents

Meanwhile, we helped many new parents to grow through their transition together.

Our personal work became an inspiration for others as our refining modality offered a beacon of hope to couples who clearly love so deeply.

Once my husband and I began to adapt and thrive in our new norm, we expanded our capacity to both guard and guide childhood from the foundational knowledge gathered through research and work experience to include intuitive awareness.

It became common sense to apply concepts such as "faster does not equal better", "more does not mean better", "being social does not signify emotional well-being", "misbehaviour does not indicate a problem", "educating is not the same as parenting", for example.

We needed to keep teaching ourselves to focus praise on effort or joy rather than the result of what our child does. We keep remembering to express "I love your father/mother in you" in more ways than words could.

We needed to choose authenticity over perfection in how we are, and humility by admitting mistakes and saying sorry. In so doing, we pray that our child learns to embrace her identities, and know deep down that all parts of her have a place at home.

As human development consultants, we make it our mission and life's work to enable the best holding structures for growth. Childhood calls for, and eventually grows to be, the most crucial holding structure a person could ever have.

Anything can be done at the expense of healthy flow in human development. Hence, engendering a deep appreciation for any trade-offs or price paid in the childhood set up is critical, because this mode of living supports the opening up of space for an immersive and expansive childhood, and this lays the foundation for immersive and expansive living in adulthood.

Conscious Parents

Conscious parents are particularly hard on themselves and parenting is one "job" where we need to really tune in, in order to sense and receive positive or helpful feedback.

I found many parents beating themselves up for doing "the wrong thing", and often desiring to do "the right thing", without seeing the tremendous opportunities for growth in all parties and work in that direction, regardless.

I often get asked by parents, "What would you do?" and "What should I do?"

In the past, my answer would have been, geared towards my opinion about what is appropriate according to me and the body of research.

Increasingly, my answers have been gearing towards enabling both parent and child to know their identities and allow choices to arise that could lead to new creation, to new ways of sensing, being and responding.

This is what growing each other's Whole Capacity is about. If we try to do what we think is right all the time, we leave no room for developing in others the capacity for growth.

Parenting affords tremendous opportunity for this, but it also brings challenges that do not show up in the same way in other contexts.

It is more helpful to leave past judgments behind in the past, and focus on bringing what is healthful and life-giving into any situation that life will continue to present.

Coming from a place of fullness in one's heart, one can lead others there too. The work is within, and starts from a place of love for oneself.

Reflection Points

1. *Try seeing the world through the eyes of the child when the child is interacting with an adult. Notice what you experience. There is no right or wrong, just different consequences. The act of noticing often brings a resolution to a situation on-the-spot. More importantly, it brings attention to one's own stage of growth, which is more sustainable than holding on to judgments of rightful or wrongful doing.*

2. *Is the adult communicating adult privileges by putting himself in a superior position?*

   Notice the difference between stating "you can have coffee when you are a bit older" or "you can drink this (alternative drink) now" plainly in a matter-of-fact way, versus saying "oh wow, what an adult you are, drinking coffee" as the child drinks milk from a coffee mug. The first states a clear respectful boundary, while the second blurs it and praises the child for drinking "coffee".

   Notice your own response to what has just been stated above. Is there judgment? Why?

3. *Is the adult communicating love and respect for all of life, just for the sake of it as a way of being?*

   Notice the difference between stating, "You can pluck the wild flowers but not this one as it belongs to someone else", versus "have you asked and listened before you pluck them?"

Notice the difference between stating "I know you like it but you can also leave it alone (instead of taking, buying or bringing it home), versus "don't do that or no you can't have it".

Notice the difference between stating, "Don't waste water" versus "Water is precious".

4. *Is the adult communicating self-love and acceptance through praising effort instead of result?*

Notice the difference between exclaiming "Excellent, good girl, you finished your food!" versus "Wonderful, you tried something new/healthy".

Notice the difference between "Good boy, you did it all by yourself!" versus "You tried and you got it!"

Notice the difference between exclaiming, "Why are you screaming?" versus "Oh my, you are feeling frustrated/angry!"

There is no clear right or wrong answer; no one answer is always the better one. The act of noticing can bring about resolution to the situation on-the-spot and calls attention to one's own stage of growth. This is far more sustainable than holding on to judgments of rightful or wrongful doing.

IN CLOSING

I hope that you have found gems that are uniquely yours as you absorbed the content of this book.

I am always keen to hear your reflections and how you have used the gems in your applications.

Write me at adele@wholecapacity.com.

I may not get a chance to personally reply to each email but I definitely read all.

BIBLIOGRAPHY

General

Ajahn Sumedho. Sound of Silence. Massachusetts: Wisdom Publishing, 2007.

Ajahn Sumedho. The Mind and The Way - Buddhist Reflections on Life. Massachusetts: Wisdom Publishing, 2011.

Bohm, David. On Creativity. NewYork: Routledge, 2004.

Brown, Brene. The Gift of Imperfection - Let Go of Who You Think You're Supposed to Be and Embrace Who You Are. Minnesota: Hazelden Publishing, 2010

Carey, Nessa. The Epigenetics Revolution - How Modern Biology is Rewriting our Understanding of Genetics, Disease and Inheritance. US: Columbia University Press, 2012.

Chopra, Deepak. SynchroDestiny - Harnessing the Infinite Power of Coincidence to Create Miracles. California: Rider & Co., 2004.

Cousens, Gabriel. Spiritual Nutrition. North Atlantic Books, California, 2005.

Csikszentmihaly, Mihaly. Flow - The Psychology of Optimal Experience. US: HarperCollins Publishers, 2008.

Davies, Morton D. Game Theory: A Nontechnical Introduction, 1997.

Dyer, Wayne. The Power of Intention - Learning to Co-Create Your Own World. US: Hay House, 2005.

Eden, Donna and Feinstein, David. Energy Medicine - Balancing Your Body's Energies for Optimal Health, Joy, and Vitality. New York: Penguin, 2008.

Frankl, Viktor E. Man's Search for Meaning. Massachusetts: Beacon Press, 2005, first published 1956.

Gladwell, Malcolm. The Tipping Point - How Little Things Can Make a Big Difference. US: Little, Brown and Company, 2002.

Grimes, Ronald. Deeply Into the Bones - Re-inventing Rites of Passage. California: University of California Press, 2000.

Grof, Christina. The Thirst for Wholeness - Attachment, Addiction and the Spiritual Path. New York: Harper Collins, 1993.

Grof, Stanislav and Grof, Christina (Editors). Spiritual Emergency - When Personal Transformation Becomes a Crisis. NewYork: Penguin Putnam, 1989.

Grof, Stanislav. Psychology of the Future - Lessons from Modern Consciousness Research. New York: State University of New York Press, 2000.

Hausner, Stephan. Even if it Costs Me My Life - Systemic Constellations and Serious Illness. New York: Gestalt Press, 2011.

Hay, Louise. You Can Heal Your Life. US: Hay House, 1984.

Hill, Gareth S. Masculine and Feminine- The Natural Flow of Opposites in the Psyche. Massachusetts: Shambala Publications, 2013.

Houston, Jean. The Wizard of Us - Transformational Lessons from Oz. New York, Atria Books: 2016.

Judith, Anodea. Eastern Body, Western Mind - Psychology and the Chakra System As a Path to the Self. New York: Crown Publishing, 2004.

Keynes, Randal. Creation - Darwin, His Daughter & Human Evolution. New York: Penguin, 2001.

Linden, David J. Touch - The Science of Hand, Heart, and Mind. UK: Penguin Random House, 2015.

Linden, David. Pleasure - How Our Brains Make Junk Food, Exercise, Marijuana, Generosity, and Gambling Feel So Good. US: One World, 2010.

Mayer, Michael. Energy Psychology: Self-Healing Practices for Bodymind Health. California: North Atlantic Books, 2009.

McTaggart, Lynne. The Intention Experiment - Use Your Thoughts to Change the World. London: Harper Element, 2008.

McTaggart, Lynne. The Bond - ConnectingThrough the Space Between Us. London: Hay House, 2011.

McTaggart, Lynne. The Field. London: Element, 2001.

Minett, Gunnel. Exhale: An Overview of Breathwork. Cambridge, UK: Floris Books, 2004.

Moorjani, Anita. Dying to be Me - My Journey From Cancer, to Near Death, to True Healing. US: Hayhouse, 2012.

Paulson, Genevieve. Kundalini and the Chakras - Evolution in this Lifetime. Minnesota: Llewellyn Worldwide, 2006.

Peabody, Susan. The Art of Changing - Your Path to a Better Life. Berkeley: Celestial Arts, Crown Publishing Group, 2005.

Peck, M. Scott. The Road Less Travelled - A New Psychology of Love, Traditional Values and Spiritual Growth. New York: Touchstone, 2003, first published 1978.

Severinsen, Stig Avall and Goldsmith, Mark Colberg. Breatheology - The Art of Conscious Breathing. Florida: Idelson-Gnocchi, 2010.

Sogyal Rinpoche. The Tibetan Book of Living and Dying. New York: HarperOne, 2002.

Sparks, Tav. Movie Yoga - How Every Film Can Change Your Life. California: Hanford Mead Publishers, 2009.

Steiner, Rudolf. Knowledge of the Higher Worlds - How is it achieved? Forest Row, UK: Rudolf Steiner Press, 2009 reprint of first English publication in 1923.

Stevens, Jose. Transforming your Dragons - How to Turn Fear Patterns into Personal Power. US: Bear & Company, 1995.

Suzanne, Kristen. Raw Awakening - Your Ultimate Guide to the Raw Food Diet. California: Chronicle Books, 2012.

Tanzi, Rudolph and Chopra, Deepak. Super Genes: Unlock the Astonishing Power of Your DNA for Optimum Health and Well-Being. Berkeley: Crown Publications, 2015.

Thich Nhat Hanh. The Heart of Understanding. California: Parallax Press, 2005.

Thich Nhat Hanh. The Miracle of Mindfulness - An Introduction to the Practice of Meditation. Massachusetts: Beacon Press, 1976.

Thich Nhat Hanh. Understanding our Mind - 51 Verses on Buddhist Psychology. California: Parallax Press.

Villaraza, Pi. Conscious Trance - The Journey to the Dancer Within. Palawan, Philippines: Still Mountains Publishing, 2010.

Walsch, Neale Donald. The Complete Conversations with God - an uncommon dialogue. NewYork: Hampton Roads Publishing Company, 2005.

Wilber, Ken, Patten, Terry, Leonard, Adam, Morelli, Marco. Integral Life Practices - A 21st-Century Blueprint for Physical Health, Emotional Balance, Mental Clarity, and Spiritual Awakening. Boston and London: Integral Books, 2008.

Wilber, Ken. A Theory of Everything: An Integral Vision for Business, Politics, Science and Spirituality. Massachusetts: Shambala Publications, 2000.

Woolger, Roger J. Healing Your Past Lives - Exploring the Many Lives of the Soul. Colorado: Sounds True, 2010.

Yalom, Irvin. Love's Executioner and Other Tales of Psychotherapy. New York: Basic Books, 2012.

http://www.innerdanceprocess.org/process.html
http://www.3ho.org/
http://www.spiritvoyage.com/

Business

Axelrod, Richard H, Axelrod, Emily M, Beedon, Julie, Jacobs, Robert W. You don't have to do it Alone - How to Involve Others to Get Things Done. California: Berrett-Koehler, 2004.

Bridges, William. Transitions - Making Sense Of Life's Changes. Massachusetts: Dacapo Lifelong, 2004.

Cowie, Kate. Finding Merlin - A Journey for the Human Development Journey in Our New Organisational World. Croydon: Marshall Cavendish, 2012.

Crofts, Neil. Authentic - How to Make a Living by Being Yourself. West Sussex: Capstone, 2003.

Flowers, Betty Sue, Scharmer, C.Otto, Jaworski, Joseph and Senge, Peter M. Presence: Exploring Profound Change in People, Organizations and Society. New York: Double Day, 2005.

Green, Stephen. Good Value - Choosing a Better Life in Business. London: Penguin Group, 2009.

Jaworski, Joseph. Synchronicity - The Inner Path to Leadership. California: Berrett-Koehler, 2011.

Lafair, Sylvia. Don't Bring it to Work - Breaking the Family Patterns That Limit Success. California: Jossey-Bass, 2009.

Nair, Chandran. Consumptionomics - Asia's Role in Reshaping Capitalism and Saving the Planet. Asia: John Wiley & Sons, 2013.

Pink, Daniel. Drive - The Surprising Truth About What Motivates Us. USA: Riverhead Books, 2011.

Scharmer, C. Otto. Theory U - Leading from the Future as it Emerges. California: Berrett-Koehler, 2009.

Scharmer, C.Otto. Leading from the Emerging Future - From Ego-System to Eco-System Economies. California: Berrett-Koehler Publishers, Inc, 2013.

https://www.presencing.com/

Relationships

Adams, Kenneth. Silently Seduced: When Parents Make Their Children Partners - Understanding Covert Incest. Florida: Health Communications, 1992.

Argov, Sherry. Why Men Love Bitches - From Doormat to Dreamgirl - A Woman's Guide to Holding Her Own in a Relationship. US: Adams Media, 2002.

Berne, Eric. Games People Play - The Basic Handbook of Transactional Analysis. US: Random House, 1964.

Broughton, Vivian. In the Presence of Many - Reflections on Constellations, Emphasising the Individual Context. Somerset: Green Balloon Publishing, 2010.

Charles, Amara. The Sexual Practices of Quodoushka - Teachings from the Nagual Tradition. Vermont: Destiny Books, 2011.

Chia, Mantak. Healing Love through the Tao - Cultivating Female Sexual Energy. Vermont: Destiny Books, 2005.

Davis, Michele Weiner. The Sex-Starved Marriage - Boosting Your Marriage Libido: A Couple's Guide. New York: Simon & Schuster, 2003.

Deida, David. Intimate Communion - Awakening Your Sexual Essence. Florida: Health Communications, 1995.

Easton, Dossie and Hardy, Janet W. The Ethical Slut - A Practical Guide to Polyamory, Open Relationships & Other Adventures. California: Celestial Arts, 2009.

Estes, Clarissa Pinkola. Women Who Run With the Wolves - Myths and Stories of the Wild Woman Archetype. NewYork: Ballantine Books, 1997.

Gilbert, Elizabeth. Commitment - A Love Story. London: Bloomsbury Publishing, 2010.

Hellinger, Bert. Acknowledging What Is. Arizona: Zeig, Tucker & Co., 1999.

Hellinger, Bert. Love's Hidden Symmetry. Zeig, Tucker & Co., Arizona, 1998.

Hogan, Eve. How to Love Your Marriage - Making Your Closest Relationship Work. California: Hunter House, 2005.

Jwala and Smith, Robb. Sacred Sex. California: Mandala, 1993.

King, Kara. Power of the Pussy - Get What You Want From Men: Love, Respect, Commitment and More! US: CreateSpace Independent Publishing Platform, 2012.

Lai, Hsi. The Sexual Teachings of the White Tigress - Secrets of the Female Taoist Masters. Vermont: Destiny Books, 2001.

Morin, Jack. The Erotic Mind - Unlocking the Inner Sources of Passion and Fulfillment. US: Harper Perennial, 1996.

Peabody, Susan. Addiction to Love - Ovrecoming Obsession and Dependency in Relationships. Berkeley, Celestial Arts, Crown Publishing Group, 2005.

Soul, Mr. Amari. Reflections of a Man. California: Black Castle Media Group, 2015.

Sperling, Vatsale and Ehud. A Marriage Made in Heaven - How to Find and Keep a Spiritually Satisfying Relationship. California: Ten Press, 2000.

Stubbs, Kenneth Ray (Editor). Women of Light - The New Sacred Prostitute. California: Secret Garden, 1994.

Stubbs, Kenneth Ray. Sensual Ceremony. California: Secret Garden, 1993.

Tatkins, Stan. Wired for Love - How Understanding Your Partner's Brain and Attachment Style Can Help You Defuse Conflict and Build. California: Harbinger, 2011.

Welwood, John. Journey of the Heart - The Path of Conscious Love. New York: Harper, 1990

Parenting

Blythe, Sally Goddard. The Genius of Natural Childhood - Secrets of Thriving Children. Gloucestershire, UK: Hawthorn Press, 2011

Bryson, Tina Payne and Siegel, Daniel. The Whole-Brain Child - 12 Proven Strategies to Nurture Your Child's Developing Mind. New York: Bantam Books, 2012.

Dancy, Rahima Baldwin. You Are Your Child's First Teacher. New York: Random House, 2012.

Khan, Salman. The One World Schoolhouse - Education Reimagined. London: Hodder & Stoughton, 2013.

Kohn, Alfie. Unconditional Parenting - Moving from Rewards and Punishments to Love and Reason. New York: Atria Books, 2005.

Medina, John. Brain Rules for Baby- How to Raise a Smart and Happy Child from 0 to 5. Seattle: Peer Press, 2014.

Miller, Alice. The Body Never Lies - The Lingering Effects of Hurtful Parenting. New York: W.W. Norton & Company, 2005.

Miller, Alice. The Drama of the Gifted Child - The Search for the True Self. New York: Basic Books, 2007 (first published in German in 1979).

Mongan, Marie. Hypnobirthing - The natural approach to safer, easier, more comfortable birthing - The Mongan Method. Florida: Health Communication, 2015.

Pantley, Elizabeth. The No-Cry Sleep Solution. Gentle Ways to Help Your Baby Sleep Through the Night. US: McGraw-Hill, 2002.

Payne, Kim John and Ross, Lisa M. Simplicity Parenting - Using the Extraordinary Power of Less to Raise Calmer,

Happier, and More Secure Kids. New York: Random House, 2010.

Perrow, Susan. Healing Stories for Challenging Behaviour. Gloucester: Hawthorn Press, 2008.

Peter, Selg. Unbornness - Human Pre-Existence and the Journey Toward Birth. Great Barrington: SteinerBooks, 2010.

Petrash, Jack. Understanding Waldorf Education: Teaching from the Inside Out. UK: Floris, 2003.

Pink, Daniel. A Whole New Mind - Why Right-Brainers Will Rule the World. New York: Riverhead Books, 2006.

Rosback, Susie, Coulson, Natalie. A Inspiring Play Spaces - Supporting Creativity Through Open-Ended Learning Environments. UK: Featherstone, 2015.

Salter, Joan. The Incarnating Child. Melbourne: Hawthorn Press, 1990.

www.ingramcontent.com/pod-product-compliance
Lightning Source LLC
Chambersburg PA
CBHW031111080526
44587CB00011B/930